ROAMING NORTHWEST GEORGIA

A Seven day tour of beautiful Rome, Georgia and surrounding area.

To Mike –
Happy Reading!,

Elizabeth Oliver Wooten

Elizabeth Oliver Wooten

DEDICATION

This book is dedicated to my husband
Thomas E. Wooten

Many of the photographs in this book are the work of Thomas E. Wooten

Comments

I read "Roaming Northwest Georgia" expecting it to be a travel guide for a week's vacation in and near Rome, Georgia. The book is much more than a travel guide. It provides a geographical study of Rome, Floyd County, and much of the surrounding area. There are daily history lessons for those who choose to follow this guide. You will find information about Native Americans, the founders of Rome, the Civil War, a president's wife with family roots in Rome, the founding of Berry College, and the building of a power generating plant at Rocky Mountain. All of this is found in this book – and much more.

Steve Johnson, Educator

With a husband who had rather stay at home than go on a vacation, I was elated to find that we could do both! This book offers excellent suggestions for visiting local sites and learning local history. Don't roam Rome without it.

Jane Davis

This book gives an excellent plan for entertaining visitors to this area.

Jason A. Morrow

TABLE OF CONTENTS

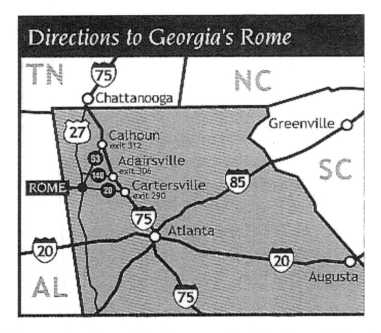

Welcome to Georgia's Rome and   Northwest Georgia

Rome and Floyd County are located in the rolling foothills of the Appalachian Mountains in Northwest Georgia. We're located in the center of a triangle formed by Birmingham, AL – Atlanta, GA – Chattanooga, TN, a little more than an hour's drive from those cities. Rome is a city that takes pride in its past, plans for the future, and delights in entertaining you. Our quality of life is so fine that we believe we have the best of both worlds, big city services and a small town friendly atmosphere. Southern hospitality abounds beginning with the people at the Tourist Center. Make this you first stop on you tour of our beautiful city.

Rome's downtown is a delightful part of history. Graceful old style lamp posts, benches, trees, quaint restaurants, and interesting shops are all a part of present day Rome. The Guide to Attractions (Chapter X) gives places to visit, more information, and ideas of things to do. It tells you were the places located, also what's happening and where. We know you will enjoy your tour of our town.

ROME, GEORGIA
STREET MAP OF BETWEEN THE RIVERS
HISTORIC AREA

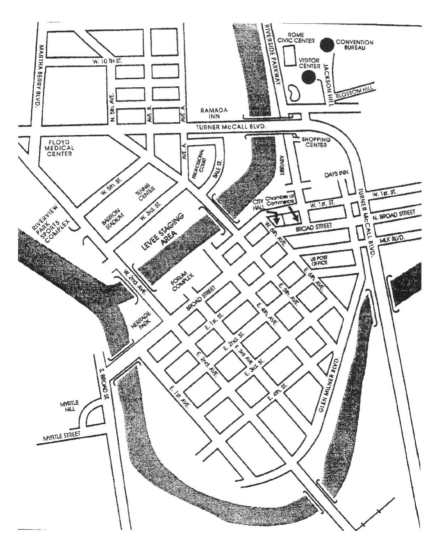

Mid pleasures and places
Though we may roam…"

John Howard Payne

Some people prefer to never leave their home, especially those who live in beautiful Rome, Georgia, and thus do not go on vacation. How would you like to have a vacation without the difficulties of getting ready for it? No reservations to make, no packing, no plane tickets to purchase, no mail and paper to stop, no phone numbers to leave, no family and neighbors to inform, no prescriptions to get, no pets to leave, and on and on of things most important – THAT YOU MUST NOT FORGET.

How you ask? This book gives you plans for a week of fun, entertainment, relaxation, and good food within walking or driving distance of your home. {Sleep in your own bed every night.} Rome and Floyd County Georgia and the Northwest Georgia Mountains promise a week that you will remember as hassle free. If you live here I promise a new look at favorite places, also things you haven't seen and things you haven't done before. If you live in the surrounding area, what's an hour or two drive in such lovely country.

I have planned seven days of relaxed enjoyment for the family, or invite a friend or two instead. Spring, summer, or fall is the perfect time to vacation here. Summer or winter may not be as enjoyable for all the day trips but most can be taken in any order. One full week, a day each week of the summer or whatever fits you schedule. We have included some suggestions for most of your meals. Also plans for two alternate days might appeal to you. Remember this is a 'NO HASSLE' vacation just for you.

CHAPTER I

DAY I

HISTORIC DOWNTOWN-
BEGIN AT THE TOP

"Where the rivers meet and the mountains begin
Where downtown is the heart of it all."

copied

Where else to begin, but at the middle of Floyd County in downtown Rome. Let's start at the top of the Clock Tower and see much of the city and county from there. This interesting piece of Rome's history is located on Clock Tower or Neely Hill at East Fifth Avenue and East Second Street. Parking is available off E. Second Street. You need a clear sunny day for this. The Clock Tower Museum is open by appointment, call the Rome Convention & Visitors Bureau, 706 295-5576 or 800 444-1834 to schedule your visit. Inside you may climb the one hundred and seven steps and look out over the surrounding mountains and all seven hills of the city plus much more.

First, you are on CLOCK TOWER HILL, also named NEELY HILL. When you finish the climb and stand looking at the Old County Courthouse clock, to your left you will see MYRTLE HILL; to your right is JACKSON HILL, BLOSSOM HILL, and LUMPKIN HILL. Continue around the circle to your right and pick out OLD SHORTER HILL on Third Avenue, and farther out is MT AVERTINE HILL off South Broad. The plaques and maps at each post on the viewing deck will help you pick out many familiar places.

The Historic Downtown part of the city is below you. The rivers, surrounding hills and mountains in the distance spread out all around you. Two rivers, the Etowah and Oostanaula flow from different directions to unite and become the Coosa River, which continues on to a new destination. Winter or early Spring with no green leaves on the trees allows you to see the rivers and historic places more clearly. There is much to be seen anytime so don't forget your cameras.

Floyd County was created in 1832 through the Cherokee Land Lottery. The land lottery gave the state and citizens of Georgia land which the Cherokee Indians had owned, before their removal from this area. In 1834 the city of Rome was founded. The original plat, (Copy on last page of book) laid out and drawn by D.R. Mitchell, dated 1834, shows Broad Street as 132 feet wide. It shows streets from Maiden Lane (Third Avenue) on the South end to about Turner McCall on the North end. The West side ends at the Oostanaula River and the West extends almost to the Etowah River. This is the area you can view from the Clock Tower and is now considered the Downtown Historic District.

The tall brick tower hides the sixty-three foot high tank which held 250,000 gallons of water and served the people of Rome from 1872 until 1893. Water was pumped from a nearby well up Bridge Street (Fifth Avenue today) to the reservoir. The water tank is built of ten-foot sheets of iron, manufactured at the Noble Foundry in Rome. The red brick, ten-sided decagon shaped tower is constructed of locally crafted brick. The forty-one-foot-high wooden structure atop the brick tower holds the clock's four faces. Each face is nine feet in diameter, the minute hand is four feet and three inches, and the hour hand three feet and six inches long. The bronze bell (32" by 40") built in 1872 still sounds the hours. The original clock works are on display in the center of the museum.

Back down the winding steps to visit the Clock Tower Museum inside the twenty-six foot diameter steel tank. On the circular tank walls are ten life size murals designed and painted by local artist Chuck Schmult. They represent the Native Americans, the Founding of Rome, the Steamboat Era, the Civil War, When Cotton was King, Charles 'Banty' Jones, The Medical History of Rome, The City Hall, and The Rome-Floyd County Library. A short video and audio available in the museum gives information about each topic. Artifacts of each time period are also displayed in the museum.

The Clock Tower is now over 130 years old and has been placed on the National Register of Historic Places. More than one million hours of history have passed since a clock was placed here and it continues to mark the minutes and hours of our lives.

ROME CITY CLOCK, *official emblem of Rome, GA*

This hill is also named Neely Hill in honor of the school that stood next to the Clock Tower. This was the first public school in Rome. As early as 1875 the subject of public school for the children of Rome was discussed, though no serious considerations of the matter occurred until 1881. Rome's Mayor, Major Samuel Morgan, and council adopted a resolution asking that a bill be introduced in the Georgia Legislature looking to establish a local school system. During the session of 1881 a provision, which required that two-thirds of the voters of the city should vote in favor of the establishment of a public school system, was passed. The vote on December 5, 1881 was 202 for public school and 107 against. It was not until May 1, 1883, when the vote was 349 for public schools and 52 against public schools, that the bill was finally passed. Col. Daniel S. Printup, the Mayor of Rome at that time, and the council passed the ordinances establishing a public school system and levied the necessary taxes.

On July 18, 1883 the city council donated a lot located on Lowes Hill (this hill has lots of names) the site of the City Clock and Water Tower, to the School Trustees as a site for the first public school building. The contract for the erection of the main building was awarded to W. D. Breckenridge on November 15, 1883. The total cost was to be $9,500. In December, the plans called for the thickness of the walls to be increased at a cost of $350 and on that day the formal contract was signed. The cornerstone of the building was laid on December 29, 1883 with much fanfare. Other items, including $1,009.50 for desks, brought the total cost to $11,483.50. The work was completed "in strict accordance with the plans and specifications" of the contract by October 1, 1884.

The school, first called Tower Hill School and then changed to Central Grammar School and later Neely School, held classes for First through Eighth grades from 1884 or 1885 until the 1950's. Many Romans remember attending here and did not want it torn down. Members of the Art League of Rome tried to have it restored as an art center and museum. In spite of their efforts, after standing seventy-six years the building, was torn down. The Rome News Tribune of Sunday, July 16, 1961 reports that the cornerstone of the old Neely School was removed Friday afternoon. Without fanfare, so unlike the Thursday afternoon in 1883 when much of the citizenry turned out for ceremonies marking its installation. The contents of the small copper box, which held the history of the past, now had crumbled to pieces. All that remained were copies of the Rome Daily Bulletin, the Rome Daily Courier and the Atlanta Constitution, along with a lone copper penny minted in 1883. The cornerstone itself was given to Mr. B. F. Quigg, who served many years as the Rome School Superintendent. On October 20, 1995 the cornerstone was replaced in its original place on Clock Tower Hill with a Commemorative Plaque. Mr. Quigg returned it and wanted it put back in the lovely park that had replaced the Neely School building.

The Jaycees have raised more than $80,000 to repair the brick structure of the clock tower and provide landscaping for the grounds. In 1995 they also helped to restore the original clock works and placed it in the museum. The park has benches and trees placed there in memory of local people. It is maintained by the City of Rome.

Time to begin your walking tour of Downtown Rome. Leave your car in the parking area of the Clock Tower Park and descend the steps to Fifth Ave. Two blocks downhill is Broad Street, one of the widest streets in Georgia. There are many shops and restaurants in this restored six-block area. I'm sure you will find time to stop at many of these.

The first Historic building you will see is at the corner of Fifth Avenue and Broad Street. The Forrest Hotel building has been restored to become apartments. The Lobby, Ballroom, and Social Room are once again functional and beautiful. They are used for social events such as weddings and other special occasions.

Before you stop to eat turn right at the corner of Fifth Ave. and Broad St. After walking past the parking area you will find The Victorian Tea Room, a lovely place to have lunch later. In the same block at 528 Broad is the DeSoto Theater. Stop to view this classic Revival Architecture, built in 1929 at a cost of $110,000. This was the first movie house in the Southeast designed specifically for sound. It's electrical equipment was the same as that used in New York City's famed Roxy Theater. The restored DeSoto Theater is presently the home of the Rome Little Theatre, a community performing group.

Continue to the corner of Sixth Ave. and cross Broad St. to visit City Hall located at 501 Broad Street. The monument on the lawn is a tribute to Dr. Robert Battey, Rome's greatest surgeon of his time. Dr. Battey achieved national prominence for his abdominal surgical techniques during the 1800's. Many of his techniques are still taught today.

The architect, who designed City Hall, A Ten Eyck Brown of Atlanta also designed the Forrest Hotel building at 436 Broad Street. City Hall, built in 1915-1916, still serves as Rome's municipal offices. It also contains the City Auditorium where many performances are held. It is home to the Rome Symphony Orchestra, the oldest symphony in the South.

In front of City Hall is the "Capitoline Wolf" statue with Romulus and Remus. This replica of the original Etruscan art of Rome Italy was an official gift to Georgia's Rome from the Roman Governor, by order of the Italian Dictator, Benito Mussolini, Rome Italy in 1929. It was presented when a new industry, Chatillan Corporation opened in Rome, Georgia, originating from Chatillan Corporation in Italy. Chatillan Corporation produced rayon fabric and was a economic factor in Rome for many years.

The statue of the Wolf with twins Romulus and Remus has long been a unique part of our city. In 1933 one of the twins, no one ever knew whether it was Romulus or Remus, was kidnapped from under the Wolf. Neither the kidnapper nor the twin was ever found. Through the efforts of the Rome Rotary Club and the International Rotary, another twin was sent from Italy to replace the missing one. Most people appreciate the statue and consider it a work of art, others are sometimes offended by it. At times the babies have been diapered or the statue was draped depending on the events. When Italy declared war on the Allies in 1940, threats to destroy the statue were made and it was placed in storage for the next twelve years. On September 8, 1952 the 1500-pound statue was placed once more on its pedestal to guard City Hall.

The bronze plate on the marble base of the statue bears the following inscription:

Translation: *"This statue of the Capitoline Wolf, as forecast of prosperity and glory, has been sent from Ancient Rome to New Rome, during the consulship of Benito Mussolini, in the year 1929."*

The Capitoline Wolf Statue

The next building North of city Hall is the Carnegie Library building, one of the thirty original libraries funded by Andrew Carnegie. This building, no longer a library has been restored for use as office space for city departments. Next to the restored library building is the Rome Chamber of Commerce. Visitors need to visit there for business and industrial information.

Walk back along the West Side of Broad Street to Fifth Avenue and look to your right and see the Historic Floyd County Courthouse, located at 101 West Fifth Avenue. Built in 1892, this Romanesque style structure is also listed on the National Register of Historic Places. It is the twenty-sixth oldest courthouse in Georgia and is still in use today as offices of Floyd County. Parts of this Courthouse are reinforced with steel rails, twisted by the invading Yankee Army when they destroyed the rail lines during the Civil War. The "Flame of Freedom" on the lawn is a tribute to veterans- past, present, and future.

Walk back along the West Side of Broad Street to Fifth Avenue and look to your right and see the Historic Floyd County Courthouse, located at 101 West Fifth Avenue. Built in 1892, this Romanesque style structure is also listed on the National Register of Historic Places. It is the twenty-sixth oldest courthouse in Georgia and is still in use today as offices of Floyd County. Parts of this Courthouse are reinforced with steel rails, twisted by the invading Yankee Army when they destroyed the rail lines during the Civil War. The "Flame of Freedom" on the lawn is a tribute to veterans- past, present, and future.

Historic Floyd County Courthouse

Time to pause for lunch at one of our fine restaurants in downtown Historic Rome.   You will find, Mexican, Italian, Southern cooking, Deli-type sandwiches, and more. Relax and rest there's more to see and do.

Next stop on your tour is the Rome Area History Museum at 303-305 Broad Street. Hours are Tuesday-Saturday from 10 AM to 5 PM. Plan to spend approximately two hours viewing and reading this one. Take the journey through time and learn of Rome's history from the period of the Cherokee Indians through World War II. This museum, under the care of the Institute for Northwest Georgia History, serves as a clearinghouse for the history and culture of Northwest Georgia.

According to C. J. Wyatt, a retired physician and local historian, many cultures came together through the years to create this area as it is today. Dr. Wyatt's collections of photographs and other artifacts, and memorabilia of this region present history to be viewed. The story of the medical field and its importance to Rome is graphically displayed. Enjoy your visit here and be sure to see the gift shop.

The fountain on the outside wall of the History Museum at West Third Street and Broad Street is a memorial to a past City Commissioner. West Third Street was paved to represent our three rivers. This area was planned as an entryway to the Forum, which you will see and hear about later.

A short distance East of where you are, at approximately 13 East Third Ave. is the spot where the founders of Rome first met. At this location, ten to fifteen feet below the present street level, lies the spring around which three men, Colonel David C. Mitchell, Colonel Zachariah B. Hargrove, and Major Philip

Hemphill, met in 1834 and decided to establish a town here. Major Hemphill invited the two to his home to discuss the matter further. His house still stands today and serves as home for the President of Darlington School. Colonel William Smith and John H. Lumpkin were brought into the planning and the city was planned and named. Each founder had his own choice for a name: Rome (for the seven hills of Ancient Rome, Italy), Pittsburgh, Hamburg, Hillsboro, and Warsaw. These were placed in a hat and the name was selected by drawing Rome. Colonel Mitchell laid out the plan for the streets. His original blueprint begins streets at our present Third Avenue, not any nearer the rivers because of flooding. Thus the Cherokee Indian's "Head of Coosa" at the confluence of the Etowah and Oostanaula Rivers became the city of Rome, Georgia.

Outside in the afternoon sunshine look at Broad Street and the buildings that line both sides. The imposing Gothic Revival structure at 336 Broad Street is the second Masonic Temple built on this site. General Sherman and his troops burned the original Masonic Temple. A number of the Union soldiers, who were masons realized their mistake and sent money to Rome to help rebuild the lodge. This building was built in 1877. In April of 1886, Rome's worst flood, cresting at 40.3 feet, inundated the building with seven feet of water as well as all of Broad Street.

The main street of Rome was first paved with bricks in 1908. Most of these were made by a local company and were square rather than flat. Some of the other streets were paved with square creosoted hardwood blocks that remained until about 1927. Broad Street was paved a second time with bricks in 1911, and was first asphalted in 1927. Electric light didn't come to Broad Street until 1889. The power lines were located in the middle of this wide street. Before that gas lights provided light. Rails for the streetcars also ran down the middle of Broad Street.

Streetcars first ran through the streets of Rome on August 1, 1885. The Rome Tribune described the vehicles as "little baby street cars tripping merrily over the rails, each drawn by a pair of careless looking mules with bells strung around them. They created quite a sensation at first, like a circus". The cost to ride was a nickel. The mules were changed after a few rounds. The route was from the East Rome depot along East Second Avenue and up Broad Street to Sixth Ave. Rome Land Company purchased the system. The rail system was expanded and steam engines powered the cars until electric motors replaced the steam pumping engines in the 1890's

Broad Street from the Cotton Block to Fifth Avenue was raised approximately fifteen feet in the late 19th century because of flooding. What's below that we cannot see? I don't know! The first floor became the basement I think. This helped save the merchandise displayed at street level. Remember the original plan for the town had no streets nearer the river than Third Avenue, because of flooding from the rivers. The floods did come. In 1886 Broad Street was covered with water deep enough that Capt. Mitchell piloted his riverboat, the 'Mitchell' 90 feet in length, directly up the Street through some ten feet of water. The rivers crested at over forty feet.

Now it is time to send one of your group up the hill, three and a half blocks away for your vehicle. Riding down Broad Street toward the Etowah River Bridge, you will view other buildings erected in the late 1800's and well preserved for use today. The 100 Block of Broad, between First and Second Avenues, is Rome's most intact historic Block. During the 1870-1900 period Rome was a river port and rail center, important for the cotton trade that centered on this block. Bales of cotton were shipped by boat downstream on the Oostanaula and one-hundred-eighty miles upstream on the Coosa from Gadsen. Cotton was also transported by wagon and rail from places such as Lookout Mountain, Mentone, and surrounding counties. Cotton was brought here during the season and temporarily stored for auctions, which were held at this intersection. The majority of the structures were cotton brokerage house, warehouses, liveries, or general mercantile houses. Many of the buildings you see were built during this time.

Park your vehicle near the corner of Broad and Second Ave. On this corner is a lovely park, aptly named, Cotton Block Park, for you to sit for a spell before you decide which restaurant to visit for dinner. La Scala at 413 Broad St. has Italian Cuisine and The Partridge located at 330 Broad St. has Southern Home Style cooking, both are locally owned restaurants. Don't worry about the cost; think how much you save by staying in Rome for your vacation.

Cotton Scene, Rome, Ga.

CHAPTER II

DAY II

THE POCKET - THE WONDER OF NATURE

"Nature is but the background." Wordsworth

Let's head North from Rome on Highway 27. Pack the picnic basket, the swimsuits, suntan lotions, and the fishing gear and bait. Dress comfortably and away we go. The northern part of Floyd County is part of the Chattahoochee National Forest. This forest is one of two national forest in Georgia and covers about 750,000 acres in North Georgia. The scenery along the way is worth the drive, but there's more.

The route today turns off Hwy 27 at Armuchee onto Floyd Springs Road seven and one-half miles from Rome. We are going to the Pocket. The Pocket gets its name because it lies in a low area surrounded on three sides by steep ridges of John's Mountain and Horn Mountain. It is an area of natural beauty, with a large spring, a stream, native plants, and a wide variety of trees. The spring and stream provides cool water for wading in the hottest months. The babbling water flows over rock filled bottoms, and wood walk bridges finish the picture. A perfect place for camping, picnicking, or hiking.

The Arrowhead Wildlife Interpretive Trail is the first stop. Other areas like Keown Falls and John's Mountain Overlook, and Hidden Creek provide hiking trails and scenic view

Vicinity Map

Three and a half miles from Highway 27, on Floyd Springs Road on the right side is a historic marker. Civil War historians will want to stop to read this bit of history of the area.

One mile from there, also on the right, is the Arrowhead Wildlife Interpretive Trail. The State of Georgia purchased this 337-acre site in 1968 to educate people and to help to preserve wildlife. The wildlife trail is approximately two miles long, but can

This part of the tour can be cut short if the sun is too hot. Several observation points are found along the trail with interpretive signs explaining some of the various management practices used to benefit wildlife. This area has been extensively managed as a wildlife demonstration area since 1980. A large variety of wildlife species can be found here.

Along the easy-walking trail are signs to inform you about the life found here. Numerous impoundments, once used as hatchery ponds, occur in the area offering excellent opportunities for the viewing of wading birds, shorebirds and waterfowl. The large area of shallow water and the shoreline associated with the ponds attract great blue herons, common egrets, mallards, and ring neck ducks. Also snipe and other birds that feed on small fish and invertebrates along the shore are seen here. Wood duck nest boxes are next along the trail. They are easy to build and very well received by Woodies when placed in suitable habitat. Plans for building the boxes are available from the Wildlife Resources Division.

Gourds and houses are provided for purple martins. Martins are very beneficial because of the large amount of insects they consume. Centuries ago native Americans made the remarkable discovery that martins would nest in gourds hung aloft near their villages. The Indians valued martins because they helped keep crows from their cornfields and hawks and vultures from their animal hides as they were being dried. Early settlers were quick to adopt the custom of providing purple martins with nesting sites. Consequently, today martin gourds and apartment houses can be found in literally every city and town in Georgia. You can provide attractive houses for purple martins. The one pictured is an example that will look great in your back yard. It does need to be installed on a high pole.

Over eight species of North American birds excavate nesting holes, using cavities resulting from decay, or using holes created by other species. Many species of cavity-nesting birds have declined because of losses of this special kind of habitat. Here nesting cavities are made to look like natural holes in old growth timber for birds like the woodpecker. As you walk through the woods you may hear loud drumming-like sounds of a woodpecker that many people interpret as wood chopping. In fact, what you are hearing is a sound referred to as 'drumming' which serves as a mating call and a warning to potential avian trespassers. Rustic houses are particularly well-suited to species that are picky about the spaces they'll inhabit. Try building log looking houses like the picture to attract birds such as woodpeckers or wood ducks.

Bluebird and bat boxes are erected here for these two very beneficial birds. Bluebirds feed primarily on insects (70%) and wild fruits (30%). Plans for bluebird boxes can be picked up at the Wildlife Resources Division Office. In the eastern part of the country, all bats feed on night-flying insect pests. Bats represent an environmentally safe, non-chemical method of insect control, and bat boxes are an excellent way to help bats live in your area.

Other wildlife you may see in this protected area are white tail deer or wild turkeys. If you are lucky enough to spot one of these deer along the trail you will understand how they got their name. When alarmed or running, the deer flashes its tail up showing the solid white underside. Canadian geese are now fairly common throughout the state. Mourning doves are also found in this area. Georgia is home to large numbers of northern birds that migrate south during the cold winter months. Further along the trail the beaver lodge you will see is constructed with mud and sticks with their entrance under water. Beavers, with their webbed-feet and large, broad, flat tails, are widely recognized as skilled dam builders. Beaver dams have created many acres of very high quality wetlands in Georgia.

Stop at the Arrowhead Regional Department of Natural Resources Office across the pond for more advice on how you can help preserve our national resources. Information about native trees and plants, timber management, and controlled fire may also be obtained there.

Approximately four miles from here your road becomes Lover's Lane. Continue on to Everett Springs Road and turn left. Slow down for the curves, enjoy the scenery and look for white tail deer and wild turkeys. John's Creek flows along side the road and trout fishing is good here. You are now in the Chattahoochee National Forest. Hunting and fishing are allowed under State of Georgia regulations. Current licenses are needed and a fishing license with trout stamp is required for those over sixteen years of age.

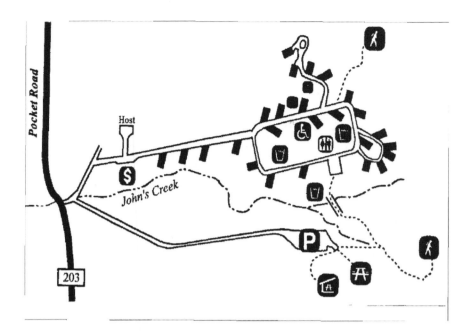

After entering John's Mountain Wildlife Area, go two and one-half miles to the Pocket's parking, picnic, and camping area. The sketch shows the parking areas, picnic tables and hiking trails. It's now time for your simple picnic lunch you packed early this morning. I hope you remembered a cooler with ice and cold drinks or you could enjoy the spring water. There is no place near here to buy food or drinks. You can walk to the picnic tables near the spring and creek from either parking area. (See sketch of area). Grills are available for cooking or heating your hotdogs.

Enjoy your food in the cool shade near the water. Wading in the cold water is fun for any age, especially after your hike. Hikers can enjoy the two and one-half-mile Pocket Loop Trail, which originates at the camp area, or the one half mile Pocket

28

Trail, which begins at the parking area to the right of the entrance. Both trails are rated 'easy'. For more hardy hikers John's Mountain Trail is nearby.

The serene beauty of the area invites you to stay awhile and relax. The stream, the bridges over it, the trees, and natural growth of the area make a beautiful background for photos. Maybe you brought your cameras and binoculars. When we visited here people were taking pictures and children were playing in the water. A lady was reading and others were enjoying a picnic lunch.

Camping and recreational vehicles are permitted in this area, but no electrical hook-ups. Hunting and fishing are allowed here with the State of Georgia regulations. Maybe there's time for some trout fishing in the cold mountain streams.

If there is time for more activities today you may want to visit the Hidden Creek Recreation Area nearby on Dry Branch. The branch appears and runs clear and cold for a day or so then disappears. This area has toilets and drinking water available. For camping each site is equipped with a picnic table, tent pad, and stone fire ring. If you are the hardy adventurous type contact USDA Forest Service, Armuchee Ranger District (706) 638-1085 for more information.

The John's Mountain Overlook and trail, as well as Keown Falls Scenic Area can be visited by car for those not up to hiking. The trail at Johns Mountain is a three and one-half mile loop. The elevation is one thousand eight hundred eighty five feet. A great scenic view from an observation deck is worth the hike. Or the Johns Mountain overlook deck is wheelchair accessible after you have driven there.

The Keown Falls trail is only one and eight-tenths of a mile to the Falls. The fifty-foot straight drop over a protruding rock ledge can be spectacular during the wet season . Excellent wildflower displays occur in the Spring and the beautiful leaf colors in the Fall are worth your trip today. Check the map for distances. We drove to the Falls and Overlook. The road was mountainous but there was no problem getting to the top. The view was spectacular and well worth going the short distance. Check the plat on the next page.

The return route back to Rome could be different. Check the vicinity map or road map. Dinner awaits you back at Mount Berry Mall area. We enjoy the variety of foods available at the Landmark Restaurant, located on Highway 27, near Martha Berry Square Mall. I hope you have enjoyed day two.

CHAPTER III

DAY III

CAVE SPRING - ANTIQUES
FISHING – LOCK AND DAM

"The turning of gears, the backwash
Of the paddle wheel, the riverboat
Bells and whistles, all sounds of A by-gone day."

Copied

Today we head South on US 411 to Cave Spring, Georgia, in the southwest corner of Floyd County. The seventeen-mile drive takes you through Vann's Valley. This fertile land was once home to Cherokee Chief David Vann, a member of the Cherokee Nation's executive council, who settled in this area in the early 1800's. Cave Spring established in 1832 is one of the most intimate and peaceful towns found in the entire South, a truly Southern town, rich in history, natural beauty and friendly people. This place invites you to enjoy a slower, more graceful way of life for a day or a weekend. With just over nine hundred residents and a single traffic light, ninety historic buildings, a natural limestone cave, a twenty-nine acre park in the heart of town, and many antique shops, there is something for everyone to enjoy.

Let's begin with a country breakfast at one of the restaurants on the square. Local people and visitors love the 'home-cookin' and hospitality at Cave Spring's family-owned restaurants. Biscuits and country ham are served Monday through Saturday, also fried catfish, pit barbeque, roasted chicken, vegetable plates, a Sunday buffet, also sandwiches and short orders make dining a casual, Y'all come back" experience. The local dinners have

31

good Southern style food, served with a smile and friendly talk about the town. The Hearn Inn has gourmet fare for the more sophisticated palate.   Cave Spring could be called the "Antique Center of Northwest Georgia". The unique shops here offer the ultimate shopping experience. Strolling through the old town square filled with many antique and gift shops brings a certain peace and tranquility to a busy life-style. The nineteenth century homes and churches that are now used for businesses create a nostalgic look for modern shoppers. In about a three-block area there are over twelve antique shops and seeking out their treasures will be an adventure for you. Cave Spring sustains a lively trade in antique furniture, glassware and crockery, jewelry, linens and curios, including an antique mall of thirty dealers.   You will be given samples of scrumptious homemade fudge at one of the shops.   Stores with names like Country Cousins sound really interesting to me.

If shopping isn't for everybody, let's explore the cave and park. The natural limestone cave and spring, which gives the town its name, is located in Rolater Park. This twenty-nine-acre park was formerly the campus of the Cave Springs Manual Labor School, later named the Hearn Academy. Early Baptist Settlers started the school in 1839. The local historical society and town government has preserved several of the school's buildings for public use. One is now a bed-and-breakfast inn. If you would like to spend the night here, call ahead for information.   The old Baptist Church that has been renovated is used for weddings and other meetings

The Hearn Inn - Cave Spring, Georgia

Caves are not my favorite place to be, but this one is different. You do not go down into it. We walked inside the mountain at ground level. The air inside was so cool that I needed a sweater, even on a hot summer day. The temperature inside stays at an average fifty-five degrees all year. My thoughts were of our Native Americans finding shelter from the cold winters and hot summers here. It's like nature's own air-conditioner. Legend has it that the native Indians held tribal meetings and games at this cave and spring site. The cave has impressive stalagmites and the legendary "Devil's Stool" formation. Call the City of Cave

Spring to check when the cave is open to the public. The spring water that flows from the cave is used to furnish water to the city and other parts of Floyd County. It has won awards for purity and taste. Be sure to have a drink.

The cave spring flows out to a serene reflecting pond and shallow stream. The pond is so clear you can see the many trout happy in the cool water. No fishing, but you can feed the fish. Also bring bread for the ducks. The kids will enjoy wading in the cool water further down the stream. The cool clear water flows on to fill a one-and-one-half acre swimming pond, the second largest in the state. Bordered by a wide grassy lawn, the complex includes a snack bar, game room and a bathhouse. The park with pavilions and picnic tables throughout is a perfect place for a picnic lunch. If it's a hot summer day, we hope you have your swimsuit and towel with you.

The Historical Society has also renovated the circa 1867 Presbyterian Church. Located a couple blocks away from the park, the church is now open to the public weekends as an art gallery operated by the local art council.

A short drive to the east of downtown is Chubbtown, one of the few communities of free blacks in pre-Civil War Georgia. Descendants of the founding family still live there.

Cave Spring has been the home of Georgia School for the Deaf, a state–operated elementary and secondary school, since 1846. The school's original administration building Fannin Hall was used as a field hospital for both Confederate and Union Troops during the Civil War.

This peaceful town with its old- fashioned, down-home atmosphere is a wonderful place to visit anytime. Special events are held during the year and include the following: Children's Trout Fishing Rodeo and Arts Festival, both held in June every year. Big Cedar Creek Arts and Crafts Festival is held in September. October brings Heritage Holiday and Christmas Open House in mid November. December brings the Christmas Parade and the town decorated for the holiday.

If it's time for lunch and you didn't pack a picnic lunch, be sure to eat at the other restaurant downtown. Enjoy your visit and shopping here before we head back to Rome, but don't tarry too long there's more to see on the route back.

Downtown Cave Spring

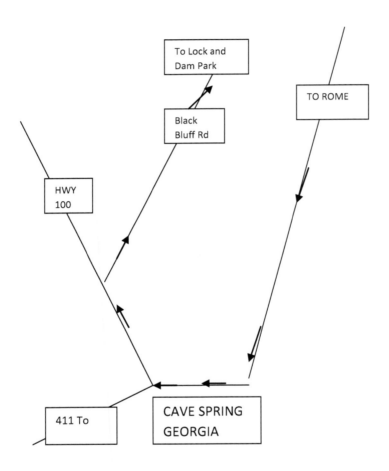

To Lock and Dam Park

TO ROME

Black Bluff Rd

HWY 100

411 To

CAVE SPRING GEORGIA

CAVE SPRING AREA MAP Follow the arrows back to Rome on Blacks Bluff Road

Now it's time to visit the Lock and Dam Park located on the Coosa River. When you leave Cave Springs continue on Highway 411 southwest for about one mile from downtown. Turn right onto GA 100 and go five miles to Blacks Bluff Road. Turn right onto Blacks Bluff Road. At this intersection, on the left is the only remaining building of a once busy community. Stop to see the Foster's Mill general Store. It has the look and smell of a general store of the early 1900's, but has been remodeled due to a fire. Enjoy a cold Coke from a glass bottle and talk with the owner-operator about what this community used to be.

The Old Foster's Mill Community dates from about 1835. The water-powered gristmill is now gone but operated for more than a century. A cotton gin here served the farmers. The Community had a Baptist Church and a Methodist Church and a school. Not far from here at that time was the county seat of Floyd County at Livingston.

Continue on Blacks Bluff Road, at the next stop sign turn right and travel approximately one mile. Lock and Dam Park will be on your left. This seventy-tree-acre public recreation area located on the Coosa River, south of Rome, offers camping, hiking, fishing, and picnicking. The Coosa River Trading Post provides fishing tackle, bait, camping items, and supplies. The park also has thirty-one fully equipped RV campsites, an area for group camping, bath houses with laundry facilities, bait and tackle shop, observation tower, nature and exercise trails, a picnic shelter, nature trails, fishing piers and a boat ramp.

In addition to being a great place to enjoy the outdoors and water, this place is interesting for the history it represents. Micajah Mayo originally owned the property and the area is often referred to as Mayo's Bar Lock and Dam. During the 1800's, before the lock and dam were built, the river was busy with steamboats and barges carrying freight, passengers, and mail between Rome and Greensport, Alabama. The boats had difficulty navigating some parts of the river with one of the worst points being Horseleg Shoals. At times temporary "dams" were devised by local citizens along the sides of the Coosa to create deeper water for navigation. Because of such problems, the U. S. Congress after years of petitioning by Georgia and Alabama Residents, began the process of making the Coosa River completely navigable. Six locks and dams were completed, the first in 1880. Construction of the current lock and dam at Mayo's Bar began in 1910 and opened for navigation in 1913, to transport steamboats over Horseleg Shoals and operated until 1941. By the time it was completed most of the large steamboats were no longer transporting goods on the rivers. The steamboats were still used for outings for church groups and hunting parties.

The lock is built of poured concrete measuring 40 X 210 feet with a nine-foot lift. Its steel lock gates were operated manually with gate struts. Gears and valves allowed water in and out of the lock. The last Lockmaster was Captain Walter F. Gray who served from 1930 until 1941 when the lock was officially closed. An upstream guide wall of poured concrete is located on the south side of the river. A poured concrete levee extends from the dam on the north side of the river. Today it's concrete walls continue to provide one of this area's more popular fishing piers.

Plans have been made to refurbish the lock to working condition at a cost of over four million dollars. Partial funding is available and most of the permits have been obtained. The lock part will be restored first and hopefully work can begin later this year. If this is done large boats can once again use the river as a passage to Alabama and as far south as the Gulf of Mexico.

Today the 73-acre regional park serves as one of the South's most popular campgrounds and fishing areas while remaining one of Floyd County's early historical landmarks. Identified historic archaeological sites associated with the lock and dam include a wharf site and a limestone quarry. The park is also listed in the U. S. Department of the Interior National Register of Historic Places. The Park hours are 7:00 AM - 11:00 PM subject to seasonal change. Call 706 234-5001 for more information and reservations.

Today would be the perfect time for a cookout for your evening meal. Rest a while, then get supplies from the Coosa River Trading Post or it's only a short distance back to Rome.

Elizabeth Oliver Wooten

CHAPTER IV

DAY IV

THE CHEROKEES - - THE MOUND BUILDERS

One generation passeth away, and another
generation cometh: but the earth abideth forever.

Ecclesiates 1:4

Today let your mind wander back to the days before Georgia's Rome. Our tour will begin at Rome's Chieftain's Museum. Don't balk at the thought of another museum, because this one is just our starting point. This former plantation house, located on the banks of the Oostanaula River, at 501 Riverside Parkway, just past Ridge Ferry Park, or between Turner McCall Blvd and Veterans Memorial Highway, was the home of Major Ridge, a Cherokee Indian Chief. A National Historic Landmark, the museum was established in 1969 by the Junior Service League of Rome. It houses many articles from the 1800's and tells the history of our Native American the Cherokee Indians and their cultural, economic, and social impact on this area.

Before we begin our tour let me give you a brief history of our early Americans.

Mississippian Culture (c700 AD to c1600 AD)

Archaeology gives us an insight into the Mississippian period of the Coosa River Valley. The Mississippian culture, also called the Mound Builders, at its apex, was the highest cultural achievement in the Southeast.

41

The dramatic social and economic changes of these people included dependence on cultivated food, political chiefdoms, and an intricately structured belief system. The Spanish Entrada of Hernando deSoto (c1540) traveled through the Chiefdom of Coosa. European contact and the diseases that followed brought an end to the Mississippian culture. I'll tell you more about these people later.

Cherokee Indians (c1700 – c1838)

The Cherokee Indian arrived in the Coosa River Valley some time after 1700. The Cherokees make a valiant effort to assimilate many of the Euro-American social and economic patterns while maintaining their traditional culture. For example, the Cherokees published a newspaper in their own language. The Ridge family, who lived at Chieftains, personified this attempt to forge the two cultures.

Agrarian South (c1834 - c1935)

With the removal of the Cherokee Indians in 1838, the dominant Euro-American culture took over the Coosa River Valley. Rome, founded in 1834 prior to the Cherokee removal, became a thriving Georgia town by the Civil War era (1861-1865). The war's impact in the region, the subsequent industrialization of the New South period and the early twentieth century are portrayed at Chieftains.

From a frontier log cabin to a Cherokee planter's house to a typical plantation, Chieftain's Museum, shows the progression of the of the history of this area. Built before Rome, about 1790 this home of Major Ridge, one of the leaders of the Cherokee Nation, has been added to many times. Inside the white two-story building, an area of the original log cabin is exposed. Many artifacts of that period are on display here. Through its architecture and the traditions shown here we learn much about this family.

I want to tell you about Major Ridge, a Chief of the Cherokee Indians, before we leave for other Indian lands. In the early 1800's he operated a thriving plantation, a country store, and a ferry that crossed the Oostanaula River at this location. He owned slaves to work the land, hired a white man to run the ferry, and was a successful businessman.

Major Ridge earned his rank, in service with the United States in the War of 1812, under General Andrew Jackson at the Battle of Horseshoe Bend. In 1814. His troops were the decisive factor in the defeat of the Creek Indians on the Coosa River in Alabama. He was instrumental in the signing of the "The Trail of Tears" treaty and like most all of the Cherokees, was forced to leave his home and go west in the 1830's. In 1839 Major Ridge, his son John Ridge a Cherokee scholar and statesman, and Elias Boudinot, were killed after arriving at their Western home by followers of Chief John Ross. His home at Chieftain's was a part of the land lottery and was given to a white man.

An interesting story was told by a lady who once lived at the old home of Major Ridge on the banks of the Oostanaula River. It was a dance at Chieftain's on a summer evening. Many guest enjoyed dancing under the stars. Music was made by two black fiddlers, the property of the owner of the mansion. Supper was enjoyed in the dining room.

"At eleven PM the guest climbed into a barge and were poled down the Oostanaula to Rome, all save the guest of the house. A lone figure drew into the shadow of a giant sycamore. It darted near the mansion, peered in with a vengeful look and was swallowed in the gloom of the nearby forest. It was an Indian woman left behind when her sister and brother redskins departed for the west, an inhabitant of a cave in the hills who had stolen down into the lowlands to gaze on the Cherokee retreat of the olden days with a prayer for the return of the tribe to its happy hunting grounds."

This reminds us of the great injustice done to the Cherokee Nation by the United States Government that removed these gentle people from our area

After seeing this interesting bit of Cherokee history, your next stop is New Echota State Historic Site or 'The Cherokee Capital', located near Calhoun, Georgia. Take Hwy 53 out of Rome, go approximately twenty eight miles and turn on 53 Spur to your left. Go east into downtown Calhoun to Hwy 41 and turn left. Go two miles and turn right onto GA 225. The site is just two miles past Interstate 75, on the right side of GA 225. (Just across the road is a golf course for those who must desert the group.)

CHIEFTAINS MUSEUM–*Home of Cherokee Chief Major Ridge.*

NEW ECHOTA

Self –Guiding Trail Map

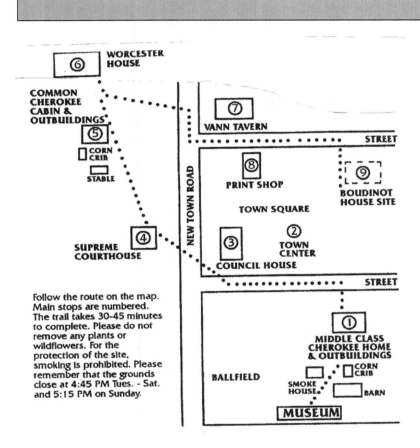

WORCESTER HOUSE ⑥

COMMON CHEROKEE CABIN & OUTBUILDINGS ⑤

CORN CRIB

STABLE

VANN TAVERN ⑦

STREET

NEW TOWN ROAD

PRINT SHOP ⑧

BOUDINOT HOUSE SITE ⑨

TOWN SQUARE

SUPREME COURTHOUSE ④

③ ② TOWN CENTER

COUNCIL HOUSE

STREET

Follow the route on the map. Main stops are numbered. The trail takes 30-45 minutes to complete. Please do not remove any plants or wildflowers. For the protection of the site, smoking is prohibited. Please remember that the grounds close at 4:45 PM Tues. - Sat. and 5:15 PM on Sunday.

MIDDLE CLASS CHEROKEE HOME & OUTBUILDINGS ①

CORN CRIB

BALLFIELD

SMOKE HOUSE

BARN

MUSEUM

New Echota, or New Town was established at the headwaters of the Oostanaula, as the capital of the Cherokee Nation. A collection of artifacts, a film, and the reconstruction of this 1819 town show the history of the Cherokee Indians. Your visit here to a reconstructed town on the same site as it was in the 1820's will show a great Indian nation as it was at that time. The Cherokees adapted to eastern civilization in a number of ways. The Council House, Supreme Courthouse, and the Print Shop help tell their story. The Cherokee National Committee met here from 1819 to 1825, until the official formation of the Nation in 1826. Dedicated missionaries who came to this area in the early 1800's helped to change the Indians way of life. Elias Boudinot and John Ridge studied at mission schools here and learned more at schools in the North. Both married white girls of prominent families and returned to their home in Georgia. John Ridge, son of Major Ridge became a lawyer and spent many months in Washington D.C. trying to help his people retain their land.

The Cherokee Nation, was the largest of the Five Civilized Tribes of the Southeast. They migrated to the Southeast from the Great Lakes Region. By 1650 they commanded more than 40,000 square miles in the southern Appalachians, covering northern Georgia and parts of four southeastern states, with a population estimated at 22,500 or more. This was their "Enchanted Land". Their Nation was a confederacy of towns; each subordinated to supreme chiefs. When encountered by Europeans, they were an agrarian people who lived in log homes, not teepees, and observed sacred religious practices.

Their religious beliefs held many of the things in nature to be sacred. The one Supreme Being was named YOWA, a name so sacred that only certain priests were allowed to say it aloud. The belief in the Great Spirit made the movement toward Christianity an easy one. A Priest was singled out from childhood for very special religious training. He was taught the use of herbs and of the sacred quartz crystals used in religious practice. The most sacred objects were kept in the council house. Very little of the ancient religion exists today. As a whole the Cherokee people have embraced the Christian religion.

The Cherokees because the first American Indian tribe with a written language thanks to the genius and hard work of Sequoyah. George Guess, known as Sequoyah, invented the Cherokee alphabet comprised of eighty-five characters. It was adopted by the Cherokee Nation and became the basis for the only Indian written language.

A newspaper, "The Cherokee Phoenix" was printed here by Elias Boudinot. Boudinot a well-traveled son of a Cherokee Chief and nephew of Major Ridge, was educated in the finest Northern and European schools. Under the leadership of editors Boudinot and later Elijah Hicks, along with two printers, the newspaper was published weekly at New Echota from 1828 until 1834. Books, 733,800 pages of the Bible, hymnals, Cherokee laws, and pamphlets were translated into Cherokee and published here. The Georgia Militia confiscated the Cherokee printing press in 1835 and carried it from New Echota.

Cherokee Syllabary

GWY ᎠᏍᏗᎠᎠᎠ

D *a*	R *e*	T *i*	� *o*	O *u*	i *v*
Ꮡ *ga* Ꮒ *ka*	Ꮄ *ge*	Ᏹ *gi*	Ꭺ *go*	Ꮒ *gu*	꭛ *gv*
Ꮵ *ha*	Ꮅ *he*	Ꭿ *hi*	Ꮃ *ho*	Ꮦ *hu*	Ꮲ *hv*
W *la*	Ꮬ *le*	Ꮅ *li*	Ꭸ *lo*	M *lu*	Ꮬ *lv*
Ꮒ *ma*	Ꮃ *me*	H *mi*	Ꮌ *mo*	Ꮍ *mu*	
Ꮎ *na*	Ꮒ *ne*	� *ni*	Z *no*	Ꮔ *nu*	Ꮕ *nv*
Ꮭ *hna*	Ꮎ *nah*				
Ꮖ *qua*	Ꮗ *qwe*	Ꮙ *qwi*	Ꮚ *qwo*	Ꮚ *qwu*	Ꮛ *qwv*
Ꮜ *sa* Ꮝ *s*	Ꮞ *se*	Ꮟ *si*	Ꮠ *so*	Ꮡ *su*	Ꮢ *sv*
Ꮣ *da*	Ꮤ *de*	Ꮥ *di*	Ꮩ *do*	Ꮪ *du*	Ꮫ *dv*
W *ta*	Ꮦ *te*	Ꮨ *ti*			
Ꮧ *dla* Ꮬ *tlu*	L *tle*	C *tli*	Ꮭ *tlo*	Ꮮ *tlu*	P *tlv*
Ꮳ *tsa*	Ꮴ *tse*	Ꮵ *tsi*	K *tso*	Ꮷ *tsu*	Ꮸ *tsv*
Ꮹ *wa*	Ꮺ *we*	Ꮻ *wi*	Ꮼ *wo*	Ꮽ *wu*	6 *wv*
Ꮿ *ya*	Ᏸ *ye*	Ᏹ *yi*	Ᏺ *yo*	Ᏻ *yu*	B *yv*

ᏍᏋ ᎤᏍᏍᏞ ᏛᎯᎭ ᏗᏣᎵᎠᎦ
ᎠᎯ ᎯᎠᎠᎠᏯ ᎦᏯᏯᎤᎠ
ᏅᏯᎠᏍᏯ ᎠᎠᎠ ᏍᎤᏯᎠ
ᏍᎮᎳᎢ ᎠᏍ ᎡᎦᎠ
ᏍᎾ ᎠᎤᏃᏯᎣ

PSALM 121:1-2

I WILL LIFT UP MINE EYES UNTO
THE HILLS, FROM WHENCE COMETH
MY HELP. MY HELP COMETH FROM
THE LORD, WHICH MADE HEAVEN
AND EARTH.

PSALM 121:1-2

The press on display now is a circa 1870 model similar in design to the original Cherokee press. During the 1954 excavations, about 1700 pieces of lead printing type were uncovered and can be seen here. Copies of an original newspaper in their alphabet are on display. In fact copies were printed in the print shop and given to us when we visited New Echota. Along side each column the same story is printed in English, so you can read the news of May 14, 1828.

In 1828, the Georgia legislature passed a law, extending their jurisdiction over the Cherokee country, and refusing to recognize their Nation as a political entity. The same year gold was discovered in North Georgia's Cherokee territory. Within a decade the Principal People's native home, their "Enchanted Land", would be there no more. This law reversed a tradition dating from 1791 of recognizing the legal sovereignty of the Cherokee Nation.

The Cherokees filed numerous lawsuits protesting encroaching settlers. Finally, in 1832 the U.S. Supreme Court ruled in favor of the Cherokees but President Andrew Jackson's refusal to enforce the ruling left the "Principle People" at the mercy of the greedy settlers and prospectors armed with the new Georgia Law. Since the situation seemed hopeless, Major Ridge led a small band of his people in the signing of the Treaty of New Echota.

Twenty-two Cherokees signed the Treaty of New Echota in the Boudinot House here on December 18, 1835. Although it was never endorsed by the Cherokee government and was considered fraudulent by many Cherokees, the treaty was ratified by Congress and used as justification to forcibly remove the Cherokees from their land in 1838. Cherokees who opposed the Treaty assassinated Elias Boudinot, Major Ridge, and his son John, after their arrival in Oklahoma in 1839.

According to this Treaty the Cherokees would forsake their land east of the Mississippi and move to Indian Territory in the West for the sum of five million dollars. In 1838 the brutal execution of the Treaty of New Echota was begun. On Saturday, May 26, 1838, more than 6,000 Federal and State troops rounded up 15,000 men, women, and children and held them in military stockades. New Echota became a prison for several hundred Cherokees who were held at Fort Wool, built near the Wochester House here. The infamous "Trail of Tears" to what is now eastern Oklahoma began in October and November 1838. More than 4,000 Cherokees died as a result of disease, exposure, and sickness during the course of capture, imprisonment, and removal. It was described by one of the survivors.

> "Long time we travel on way to new land. People feel bad when they leave Old Nation. Womens cry and make sad wails. Children cry and many men cry ..... but they say nothing and just put heads down and keep on go towards West. Many days pass and people die very much"

Recollections of a survivor

When we visited New Echota, we walked the approximate one mile trail and saw no reminders of the injustice these gentle Native Americans suffered. The birds were singing, the smell of honeysuckle, a spring of water and New Town Creek were very peaceful. A walking trail includes signs that explain the natural features of this land. We suggest you walk the trail and visit the outside buildings before you tour the museum. Be sure to visit the last house, the Worcester House, which was home to the missionaries. Rev. Samuel A. Worcester and Rev. Elijah Butler were sentenced to four years in the Georgia Penitentiary for a charge of inciting the Indians to revolt. They served one year and four months and were released on their promise to leave the State.

The Museum has air conditioning, rest rooms and guides who will tell you more if time permits. We hope you enjoy your visit to New Echota as much as we did.

Another historic site of the Cherokee Nation is located north of here on Hwy 225 near Chatsworth, GA. Take I-75 to the Dalton exit and go one mile east on Highway 76 to the intersection of Hwy 76 and Hwy 225. The Chief Vann House is called the "Showplace of the Cherokee Nation". Chief James Vann built this two-story classic brick mansion in 1804. This was the first brick house owned by a Cherokee. Decorated with beautiful Cherokee hand carvings done in natural colors of blue, red, green, and yellow, the home features a cantilevered stairway and many fine antiques. The government seized the properties because son Joseph who inherited the house unknowingly violated state law by hiring a white man to work for him. The house was awarded to a white man in the land lottery in 1834. If you don't have time to visit there today, maybe someday you will.

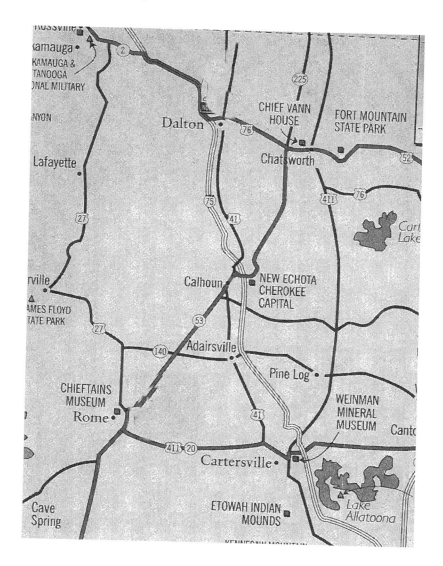

*AREA MAP FROM ROME TO CAHOUN,
DALTON AND BACK TO CARTERSVILLE,*

The next stop on today's Indian Trail is The Etowah Indian Mounds in Cartersville, Georgia. It's time for lunch at any of the many restaurants in Calhoun, Georgia.

After lunch continue South on Interstate 75 for approximately thirty miles and exit at Highway 411.

Continue on 411 South/East into downtown Cartersville, and then follow the well-marked route to the Etowah Indian Mounds. The mounds rise from a flat plain along the Etowah River. The three huge earth mounds are silent remains of where once several thousand Native Americans lived completely off the land, more than four hundred years ago. Who then built the mounds? A superior race, a people of foreign and higher civilization? Who occupied America long before the North American Indians? Could the mounds have been built by the ancestors of the very Indians whom the white man displaced?

Research proves the inhabitants of the Etowah village were part of a much larger group known as the Mississippian culture. The Mississippian Period, named because the beginnings of the culture were found along the Mississippi River, began in approximately 1000 AD. This culture was here long before the Creek or Cherokee tribes populated this area. The history of these Mound Builders, as archeologists now reconstruct it, begins soon after the beginning of agriculture in what is now the Eastern United States. No one knows whether the inhabitants were actually farmers or not. They used pottery and dug substantial storage pits for conserving winter food. They gathered a variety of vegetable foods and caught fish in the rivers. So diverse were the food resources of their environment that they may have had little need to supplement their diet by farming.

At the Etowah Indian Mounds and village site, the flat topped earthen knolls were used between 1000 AD and 1500 AD as a platform for the home of the priest/chief, or as temples and mortuary houses. Chief Priests governed their fortified towns. These leaders lived in temples atop the largest mound. Upon the death of the Chief Priest, his temple would be destroyed and another layer of earth would be added for his successor. The flat topped earthen knolls, the largest standing sixty-three feet high and covering three acres is preserved as it was when found. The mounds and site symbolized a society rich in culture and ritual. It is believed that these people enjoyed an intricate system of

trading, were accomplished craftsmen, and practiced sophisticated religious beliefs. By the time the first white settlers came to this area no trace of the Mound Builders remained except their silent earthworks.

Population centers of these people were found in other river basins as their culture was probably sustained by the cultivation of crops. Towns were subordinate to other towns with more powerful Chief Priests; thus confederacies were established. The Mississippian people, particularly the Chief Priests were of significantly larger physical stature than the European explorers who encountered them. The Creek Nation is believed to be the southeastern descendant of the Mississippian Culture.

It's now time to visit the Museum, where cold water and air conditioning await you. A short audio-visual show will give you more information about the items on display here. Many artifacts shown here were found during the excavations of Mound C and the village area. These show that the natives of this political and religious center decorated themselves with shell beads, tattoos, paint, and complicated hairdos, feathers, and copper ear ornaments. Also on display are two marble statues, two-foot tall, male and female that were found in one of the last burials made at the Mound B temple. A monolithic axe carved from a single piece of stone made me wonder how it could be done without modern tools.

In 1965 the Etowah Mounds Archaeological Area was designated a National Historic Landmark by the U. S. Department of the Interior under the Historic Sites Act of 1935. This award is reserved for sites possessing exceptional value in illustrating the history of the United States of America. The area is also listed on the National Register of Historic Places.

What happened to this advanced civilization in the 1500's? We have no written records to tell us. Hernando de Soto and his conquistadors in 1540 did record visits to people living in the southeastern United States in the sixteenth century. They visited confederacies headed by powerful chiefs. If these were the people they wrote about, the Mississippian civilization did not last long after that. Within decades, alien diseases had depopulated much of the Southeast and the economic and political structure of these people collapsed forever.

The myth of the Mound Builders was given its loftiest expression by the New England poet, William Cullen Bryant.

"And are they here-

The dead of other days – and did the dust

Of these fair solitudes once stir with life

And burn with passion? Let the mighty mounds

That overlook the rivers, or that rise

In the dim forest crowded with old oaks,

Answer, A race, that has passed away,

Built them; - a disciplined and populous race

Heaped, with long toil, the earth, while yet the Greek

Was hewing the Pentelicus to forms

Of Symmetry, and rearing, on its rock

The glittering Parthenon ...

Then enter the villains:

The red men came-

The roaming hunter tribes, warlike and fierce."

And THE MOUND BUILDERS VANISHED FROM THE
EARTH ...

W. C. Bryant

Time to head back to Rome, by way of the unique town of
Euharlee, Ga., (pronounced U'har lee). population eight hundred
and fifty. It's ten miles from the Mound area but it's on the route
home and well worth looking for. I'm not sure of it's Indian
history but it's a turn of the century town.

Retrace your route to the stop sign at Old Mill Road, turn left
until you find Hwy 113 and at the next red light turn right to New
Euharlee Road. After you cross the Etowah River look for
Covered Bridge Road and turn left onto it. A short distance you

will find the two churches, fire station, and a country store that make up the town. Be sure to visit the Covered Bridge at the end of the road. It is one of the few 1800's covered bridges still standing and in use as a pedestrian bridge.

Return to Chulio Road (same as New Euharlee Road, it changed names) turn left, go four miles to Macedonia Road and take a right, 3.5 miles to Hwy 411 and go left, this takes you back to Rome.

CHAPTER V

DAY V

CIVIL WAR PERIOD

...The principles for which they fought can never die.
Quote from the Confederate Monument.

No book about Rome would be complete without some facts about the influence of the Civil War on our City. Rome, by the time of this devastating conflict 1861 to 1865, was a prosperous city. Steamboats on the rivers and railroads from Atlanta and Chattanooga coming to Rome via Kingston, helped to make Rome a busy manufacturing center. Businesses such as Noble Brothers Foundry and Iron Works made this city especially valuable to the War. Hospitals and medical facilities here were an important part our city contributed, both to the Confederates and later to Union soldiers.

As early as May 1861 Rome and Floyd County were sending their best fighting men off to enlist in the Army of the Confederacy. Most of these were the young unmarried. They had no weapons of war but in all else were fully provided. Thus began four year of hardship, fear, misery, and death for many of the citizens.

A late start will be fine for today, we're not going very far. We have an interesting and easy tour driving past buildings that were not destroyed when Rome was burned by General Sherman's

Union troops on November 10 and 11, 1864. We'll visit the graves of soldiers and citizens of Rome at Myrtle Hill Cemetery. Later we'll stop on Jackson Hill to view three pieces of history and maybe take a short walk through Fort Norton near there.

Before we began our tour today you need to hear about an interesting event of the war. Even if you are not an avid Civil War historian you need to know the story of 'The Locomotive Chase". On April 12, 1862, a Rome engine, the Wm. R. Smith, played an important part in the chase and capture of twenty-two Union men who stole a Southern train. It all began when James J. Andrews, a Union spy was commissioned to lead a raid into Georgia and burn the railroad bridges between Big Shanty at Kennesaw, GA and Chattanooga, TN.

At six AM on April 12th, Capt. Wm. A Fuller, conductor of a passenger train left Atlanta headed for Chattanooga. The engine was the "General", a wood burning steam engine that carried in addition to passengers, freight from Chattanooga to Atlanta. Three empty boxcars were next to the engine for the freight on the return trip. While Capt. Fuller, the crew of the General, and the passengers were having breakfast at Big Shanty, Andrews's group of twenty-two Union men stole "The General" and three boxcars. The chase that followed covered a distance of eighty-five miles. Capt. Fuller and others first ran two miles, then used a handcar for twelve miles to Etowah. An old engine "Yonah" was on a sidetrack there. Quickly made ready and turned they used it to go the fourteen miles to Kingston GA, where they found out that Andrews and his Union men had just left in the "General". The "Wm. R. Smith" was waiting with steam up to take the Atlanta passengers to Rome, but instead took up the chase of the General for the next five miles. Four miles south of Adairsville, sixty yards of track was torn up by the Union men. Capt. Fuller and his men had to abandon the "Wm. R. Smith" and again ran another two miles. Next a freight train headed South was stopped by Capt. Fuller standing on the tracks brandishing his pistol. The next fifty miles, with the freight engine, "Texas" going backwards, brought them in sight of the stolen train. Andrews's party had cut telegraph wires, disconnected two boxcars, laid cross ties on the track and tore up rails, but had no time to blow up bridges. When they had no more wood to burn they tried to burn part of the remaining boxcar. Next they reversed the engine to bring on a collision with the "Texas" but in their haste left the brake on and there was not enough steam to back up the train.

The twenty-two Union men ran into the woods, "Every man take care of himself!" shouted Andrews, and they scattered. A group of mounted Confederate soldiers had joined the chase and were sent out after them. All were captured and some were later executed. The "General" was returned with very little damage, thanks to Capt. Fuller and many others.

The actions of Capt. Fuller and these men show the determination and courage of the people of the Confederacy. Rome had men and women who bravely protected this area.

The first stop today is at 105 Shorter Avenue to see the Darlington Lower School building. "Thornwood", the former mansion of Alfred Shorter, a Doric-columned three-story frame structure was built in 1848. The exterior has been preserved much as it looked in the nineteen century. It was occupied by Federal troops during the Civil War, but escaped major damage and today is one of Rome's most impressive antebellum buildings. This historic building is now used for grades one through five of the Darlington School.

Next go South from Rome on US 411 and exit at Darlington Drive, turn right and go about four blocks, at the intersection of

Cave Springs Drive you will see the main entrance to Darlington School. Darlington is a private school, grades kindergarten through twelve, with local students, others from many of the United States, as well as many International students. After entering the gate on the right you will view "Alhambra", Darlington School's 'Home on the Hill', used now as the home of the President of Darlington Schools. It is the oldest house in Floyd County and has served as home to five School presidents since 1923. Can you believe this house was built in 1832 by Major Philip Hemphill before the founding of Rome?

In the spring of 1834 Major Hemphill entertained three other prominent Georgian in his home at this location; Colonel Daniel R. Mitchell , Colonel Zachariah B. Hargrove, and Colonel William Smith. These four men advocated the establishment of a new town at the confluence of the Oostanaula and Etowah Rivers. To decide a name for the town they placed four names in a hat and drew out the name Rome.

Major Hemphill's house was spared the destruction of the Union troops. This historic house has served as a recreation and refreshment center for the school. It had been added to and changed through several owners until it no longer resembled the dignified structure it was designed to be. Dr. Clarence R. Wilcox, the first president of Darlington lived there from 1923 until 1955. Dr. Ernest L Wright, who succeeded Dr. Wilcox was adamant that the house be repaired. It was restored as closely as possible to its original simplicity and dignity. It is now one hundred and seventy two years old, still beautiful and still used.

Darlington School has other beautiful building. The Chapel that faces the lake is a non-denomination church. It has beautiful stained glass windows and is used for weddings and other events.

The Lake is a focal point for the campus and has long been a popular place for Rome residents and later students.

The white swans that make their home there are beautiful, I hope you will see them today. Continue your drive around the lake and see the beauty of this school campus. John Paul Cooper, a prominent Rome cotton merchant who, with his wife Alice Allgood Cooper had founded Darlington in 1905, purchased the property in 1912 and deeded the land to Darlington School in 1921. The preparatory school's leaders have received students, parents, and alumni from all over the world since that time.

'ALHAMBRA' Home of Darlington School President

This property at one time acquired the name Mobley Park. A legend that Hernando DeSoto had camped at this site during his sixteenth century exploration of Georgia gave the area the name of DeSoto Park. In the late 1890s the City Electric Railway Company bought the property as an investment and opened the area as an amusement park. Some old timers of Rome remember the trolley from town to the park where they swam, fished, and picnicked. The lake was enlarged, and spanning it was an elaborate arched bridge.

Exit at the next gate and go left on Cave Springs Drive to South Broad St. Turn left on South Broad Street, go about six blocks and you will find Myrtle Hill Cemetery on your left. Soon after Rome was established about twenty-five acres of land was purchased for a burial plot, on one of the hills of Rome now named Myrtle Hill. A plan was laid out and the first interment was in 1857. Turn left onto Myrtle Street and stop here to observe the monument of General Forrest, the monument to the Women of The Confederacy, and the grave of the Known Soldier.

MYRTLE HILL CEMETERY DIAGRAM

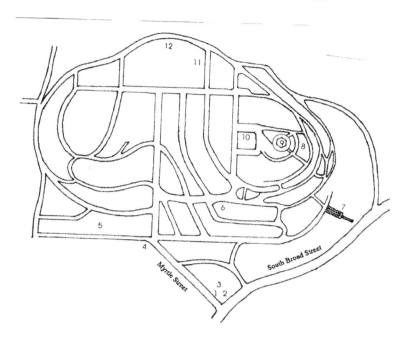

1. Statue of Gen. Nathan Bedford Forrest
2. Women of the Confederacy Memorial
3. Grave of Charles W. Graves.
4. Main Entrance to the Cemetery
5. Graves of Civil War Soldiers
6. Ellen Axson Wilson Grave
7. Steps to Cemetery with an arched marble gate.
8. Grave of Dr. Robert Battey
9. Confederate Soldier Memorial
10. Graves of Daniel Mitchell and Zachariah B. Hargrove, two of the founders of Rome
11. Burial site of Colonel Alfred Shorter
12. Grave of Daniel Printup, an early Roman.

This monument to Gen. Nathan B. Forrest was dedicated on April 3, 1909, and placed in the center of Broad Street. To lessen traffic congestion it was moved, along with the Women of the Confederacy monument, to this location on December 30, 1952. Gen. Forrest is honored, by Romans, for his role in capturing a Union raiding party led by Colonel Abel Streight. This incident of the war that was very important to Romans occurred on May 3, 1863. The engagement took place west of town and saved Rome from a Federal attack. During April and May 1863 a large army of Union forces led by Hathaway Streight had invaded Alabama and Georgia from the Tennessee side. On Sunday May 3, 1863 Gen. Nathan Bedford Forrest by his indomitable will and after a running fight of three days and nights, with 410 men, captured Col A. D. Streight's raiders, numbering 1600, thereby saving Rome from destruction. The Tri-Weekly Courier, dated May 5, 1863, reported the events of May 3rd that made Gen. Nathan Bedford Forrest and John H. Wisdom our heroes.

I have taken parts of the Courier's text to tell the story. *"Sunday morning last opened at half past two o'clock AM with an alarm. Mr. John H. Wisdom, of Gadsden, Alabama and a former resident of this city, reached here after riding with hot haste for eleven hours, and gave information, that the enemy were at Gadsden when he left, and were bound for Rome."*

Preparations were made with haste to give them a warm reception. Two pieces of artillery were placed in position, commanding the road and the bridge, and cotton barricades were erected. Dispatches from Gen. Forrest, saying he was fighting them at Gaylesville, Alabama, with an inferior force were not very promising. About two hundred of the enemy's advance troops reached the environs of the city. Learning that the city was prepared they retreated and a small but resolute band of citizens pursued them.

Meantime, Gen. Forrest had overtaken the main body not far this side of Cedar Bluff, Alabama. Gen. Forrest demanded surrender after some slight skirmishing. The entire Yankee force, consisting of 1800 men were made prisoners of war, and as this included the infantry being chased by the citizen cavalry, they too were turned into disarmed infantry. Gen. Forrest accomplished this bold feat with less than 700 men, though the rest of his command was in supporting distance. *"Such a jubilee Rome has never experienced! Such raptures over Gen. Forrest and his brave men!"* The article concluded with the statement that "the reinforcements arrived here yesterday at noon from Atlanta, but owing to the peculiar nature of existing circumstances, they will have nothing to do but guard duty."

The engraving on one side of the base of the Statue reads:

HE POSSESSED THAT RARE TACT, UNLEARNABLE FROM BOOKS, WHICH ENABLED HIM. NOT ONLY EFFECUALLY TO CONTROL HIS MEN, BUT TO ATTACH THEM TO HIM WITH HOOKS OF STEEL

WOLSELEY

You can understand why this dashing cavalryman, General Nathan Bedford Forrest, was a popular hero of the Civil War. John Wisdom is also a Rome hero who is remembered each year at the Heritage Holidays Festival in Rome. A horse and wagon ride and a parade are held in his honor every October at this event.

The next monument is to the "Women of the Confederacy". This monument was erected March 9, 1909 honoring "the memory of our heroic women of the South." It honors Rome's women for their role as nurses to both Union and Confederate soldiers in the many local hospitals set up here during the war. Rome became a center to treat the sick and wounded soldiers. Besides helping those who were ill the women of this area engaged in making uniforms and articles of clothing for the volunteers. They also carried on all the household and even farming chores, also the day to day business affairs. A quote from the Courier reported on May 5, 1863 says. "The most novel thing I have seen in some time was a woman plowing yesterday with a pistol buckled around her."

The engraving on the base of this monument reads:

1861 - 1866

TO THE WOMEN OF THE CONFERDERACY

WHOSE PURITY WHOSE FIDELITY WHOSE COURAGE

WHOSE GENTLE GENIOUS IN LOVE AND IN COUNSEL

KEPT THE HOME SECURE THE FAMILY A SCHOOL OF

VIRTURE. THE STATE A COURT OF HONOR.

WHO MADE OF WAR A SEASON OF HEROISM AND OF

PEACE A TIME OF HEALING. THE GUARDIANS OF

OUR TRANQUILITY AND OF OUR STRENGTH
WOODROW WILSON

GEN. NATHAN B. FORREST MONUMENT (FOREGROUND)
AND THE MONUMENT TO THE WOMEN OF THE
CONFEDERACY

Next let's visit the grave of Charles W. Graves: the Known Soldier of World War I. Private Graves, who enlisted on May 19, 1917, at Jasper, Tennessee was killed in action in October 1918 by an exploding German shell. A ship, the Cambria, was returning Graves body along with one thousand others on March 29, 1922, to New York harbor. It had been decided to select one of these bodies of a soldier killed in World War I, to be the Known Soldier. This soldier was to represent all of the dead soldiers of World War I and was to be buried alongside the Unknown Soldier in Arlington National Cemetery. Pvt. Graves's Mother who lived in Rome wanted her son to be buried in the Graves family cemetery, The Antioch Church Cemetery, on Callier Springs Road. The Rome News Tribune reported on April 7, 1922, the second burial, the first had been in France, of Private Graves body. It was a military funeral with much fanfare. Later the idea of having a " Known Soldier" national shrine here appealed to some very influential people. Since the American Legion was behind the project plans were soon made to move the body of Pvt. Graves again. There was difficulty getting permission to move his body once more. They got around that by moving it at night to a new grave already dug and waiting at Myrtle Hill. That third reburial took place on September 11, 1923. On November 11, 1923 an Armistice Day celebration held just nineteen days after the burial of Charles W. Graves at Myrtle Hill Cemetery, unveiled plans for a monument to be built on top of the simple marble slab, whose probable cost was estimated at $15,000. Three machine guns surround the grave and two cedar trees were planted one on either side of the grave.

In January 2000 plans were made once again to memorize Private Graves grave and the area around it. A group of citizens formed the Myrtle Hill/Oak Hill Memorial Association and they began raising funds by selling bricks to honor or memorize Veterans of all wars. The first phase of this plan was to pave the area immediately around the grave. The marble slab which surrounds this area was dedicated on November 11, 2000. The second phase of the step down area and plaques were dedicated on Memorial Day 2001. The third and final phase was completed and dedicated on Memorial Day 2002. Next the efforts of this group will focus on Oak Hill Cemetery, which was the first official City of Rome Cemetery, located near Riverside Drive and West Second Street on Lumpkin Hill

GRAVE OF PRIVATE CHARLES W. GRAVES

Rome's army hospitals, which filled many Broad Street buildings, overflowed with wounded soldiers. Many of these were buried in Myrtle Hill Cemetery. The East side, along Myrtle Street, is home to the remains of hundreds of Confederate and Federal Soldiers. This area is marked by magnolia trees, rose bushes and crepe myrtles and is in a V shape. In total there are 377 graves in this location, including eighty-one Confederate unknown and two Federal unknown soldiers. All of the graves are uniformly marked with gray marble slabs. Flags are placed on every soldier's grave for Memorial Day, Fourth of July , and Veteran's Day.

GRAVES OF CONFEDERATE AND UNION SOLDIERS

The driving entrance to the cemetery is from Myrtle Street. This drive provides a scenic tour of the cemetery's six levels as driveways branch off into smaller paths. Brick and stone walls have been built to keep the different levels from falling. Our next War memorial is at the highest point of the cemetery. This site provides an awesome view of the rivers and downtown Rome. The marble monument to the heroes of the Confederacy looks to the west of the city and consists of a confederate soldier standing at parade rest. The spirit that gave strength to the South in its adversity is stated on the pedestal of the Confederate Soldier monument in words of stark conviction.

> *"This monument is the testimony of the present to the future that these were they who kept the faith given them by the fathers. Be it known by this token that these men were true to the traditions of their country's call; steadfast in their duty faithful even in despair, and illustrated in the unflinching heroism of their deaths, the free-born courage of their lives."*

> *"They have crossed the river and sleep beneath the shade."*

> *"How well they served the faith their people know. A thousand battlefields attest, dungeon and hospital bear witness. To their sons they left but honor and their country. Let this stone forever warn those who keep these valleys that only their sires are dead– the principles for which they fought can never die."*

Look out over the city and remember those who fought here. You can view the meeting of the rivers, the Oostanula and Etowah flowing together to form the Coosa River. During 1863 and 1864 riverboats moved munitions, troops, and prisoners of war on our rivers. Just across the Etowah is the site of the Noble Foundry, on East First Ave. where the Southeastern Mills large buildings are now. James Noble, Sr. and his six sons – John Ward, Samuel, William, James, Jr., Stephen, and George staffed one of the Confederacy's busiest munitions plants.

In November of 1864 the evacuating Union Soldiers had these orders from General Sherman.

> *"You will destroy tonight all public property not needed by your command, all foundries, mills, workshops, warehouses, railroad depots or other storehouses convenient to the railroad, together with all wagon shops, tanneries, or other factories useful to the enemy; Destroy all bridges immediately, then move your command tomorrow to Kingston."*

Union forces occupied our city from May 18 till November 18, 1864. It is said the damage would have been worst except for the hospitals that might be needed later. After the Federal evacuation only forty males remained to fend off raids by renegade 'scouts' who ravaged the town until enough citizens returned to restore order in the streets of Rome. Many other businesses and homes were destroyed during the Union evacuation of November 10, 1984

Before you leave the cemetery, visit the graves of Dr. Robert Battey, a noted surgeon of his time. The Battey Mausoleum is one of the most distinctive sights in the cemetery. The graves of Daniel Mitchell and Zachariah B. Hargrove, two of the founders of Rome are located here.

Don't miss the simple headstone of Ellen Axson Wilson, wife of President Woodrow Wilson. Born in Savannah, Georgia on May 15, 1860, Ellen Louise Axson moved to Rome in March of 1866. Her father, the Rev. Samuel Edward Axson was pastor of Rome's First Presbyterian Church, where Woodrow Wilson first saw her April 8, 1883. They were married in Savannah, June 24, 1885. The Wilsons were the parents of three daughters. A gifted painter, Mrs. Wilson contributed to humanitarian causes, including The Berry Schools. As America's First Lady, she championed improved working conditions for women, African Americans and better housing for Washington's homeless. President Woodrow Wilson and Ellen had three daughters. Ellen Axson Wilson died on August 6, 1914 in The White House.

The burial site of Colonel Alfred Shorter, for whom Shorter College, Shorter Hill, and Shorter Avenue are named, and the grave of Daniel Printup, one of the founders of Myrtle Hill Cemetery can be visited on the way out. There are many picturesque and beautiful monuments and vaults in this interesting cemetery. Look for some of the hundreds of crepe myrtle bushes, which were planted here and thus, gave their name to Myrtle Hill Cemetery.

Other houses and churches still stands today that were here during the Civil War. We will visit some of these on another day. Now it's time to go to another of Rome's seven hills.

WELCOME TO ROME

Our next stop today will be Jackson Hill. The Greater Rome Convention and Visitors Bureau is located there as well as other interesting things. Reeves Station Depot, 'The Welcome Center', stands proudly on Jackson Hill, one of Rome's seven hills. The gaily-painted restored train depot should be your first stop when visiting in Georgia's Rome, Reeves Station was originally located eighteen miles north of Rome and was built in 1901 by Southern Railway. It served as a depot and Pony Express stop. In 1976 a Rome citizen rediscovered it; purchased it, moved it to Rome and gave it to the City of Rome to be used as a Welcome Center. A retired caboose was given by Norfolk Western Railway in 1984 and is connected to the depot. The things located here aren't all related to the Civil War but they are too interesting to leave out of our tour.

Also located on Jackson Hill or Civic Center Hill, as it is know now, are many interesting pieces of history. Four large plaques tell of events that begin in the late 1530's. One records the visit of Hernando DeSoto and his troops to Rome. Others are of the Civil War period and tell of the Federal occupation of Rome by General Wm. T. Sherman in 1864; of Brig. General J. C. Davis march to Rome on May 16, 1864; and information about Confederate Major General S. G. French. You must stop to read all four.

There are four other things, to see and read about, located near the plaques. The lathe on display here, built in 1847, was part of the machinery of the Noble Brothers Foundry that operated in Rome from the 1850's till 1864. Steamboat engines, furnaces, locomotives and cannon were made with the help of this giant piece of machinery. During the war the Noble Foundry produced many of the Confederate artillery pieces, and was subsequently destroyed by the Union soldiers at the end of their occupation of Rome in 1864. This enormous lathe used to fashion the cannons was so over-whelming that it could not be destroyed by the Union troops. The marks made by the sledgehammers of the soldiers who tried to destroy it are still evident on its side.

The next item on display is a Corliss steam engine that served Rome's Southern Cooperative Foundry for sixty-nine years from 1902 to 1971. The Corliss was run by sixty pounds of boiler pressure steam. The Southern Cooperative Foundry was one of many in Rome that produced stoves, heaters, ranges, and grates. Rome was called the 'Stove Center of the South.'

An Eighteenth century Cotton Gin that is on display is an invention Eli Whitney. Mr. Whitney invented the cotton gin in 1793 while living in Georgia. His gin revolutionized the economy of the American South. With the cotton gin it became easier and quicker to separate the fiber from the seed of cotton. Before his invention, Georgia produced 1,000 bales of cotton a year, but by 1860 the yield was 700,000 bales a year. This same principle with very little modification is still employed in the modern gins used today.

The Boswell Log Cabin was built about 1850 and typified the home built by pioneer families who settled on small farms between 1830 and 1850. The cabin, originally located on the Calhoun Road just inside the Floyd County line, was built by Richard Boswell and his wife, Rhoda. These early settlers were the parents of seven sons and three daughters who made their home in the cabin. The cabin was purchased, transported to Rome and placed at its present location by the City of Rome in 1973. With the exception of a new roof the cabin remains in its original state. Visitors may see this early dwelling and imagine life as it was 150 years ago.

The Rome Municipal Civic Center building, used for special events and community gatherings, is also located on Civic Center Hill. WPA (Works Progress Administration) workers built this building, constructed of native rock, in the 1930's. It is a popular place for events, from wedding receptions to Bar-B-Que cookouts. It can be rented from the City of Rome.

Take time to visit the Welcome Center where each year thousands of visitors are welcomed to Rome, GA USA. You as Romans will be as warmly greeted and you will learn more about Georgia's Rome.

In the area above here are the remains of Fort Norton.

This high hill was one of the fortifications the Confederate Forces built to protect Rome. In mid and late 1863 orders were given to construct fortifications on the hills around Rome.

African-American slaves from local farms were hired for the project. Citizens were asked to supply tools and laborers using their slaves. When this didn't bring many workers, soldiers convicted of various crimes were sentenced to work on the fortifications. Trenches or "earthworks" have been uncovered that curve around the southern and western side of Jackson Hill. Remains of a part of these can be seen going up Reservoir Hill. This area has not yet been developed into a tourist site, but plans are under way to preserve this important piece of Rome's history. The City of Rome owns the property and the Roman Legion has long promoted the preservation and restoration of Fort Norton on Jackson Hill.

Your evening is free to visit any of our fine restaurants, see a movie, or just go home.

Elizabeth Oliver Wooten

CHAPTER VI

DAY VI

BERRY COLLEGE – ROCKY MOUNTAIN STONEBRIDGE GOLF – MT. BERRY MALL

A wise man will hear and increase learning . .
Proverbs 1:5

Today you have a choice of different places to visit and different things to do. Each is an interesting place to see and you may have time for two or more. The choices include Berry College Campus Martha Berry Museum, Rocky Mountain Recreation Area, Stonebridge Golf Course, and Mount Berry Square Mall.

I suggest that you begin with a tour of the Martha Berry Museum and Art Gallery, Oak Hill, and the campus of Berry College. Consisting of 26,000 acres, this is the largest and one of the most beautiful college campuses anywhere. The Southern setting and beautifully preserved antebellum plantation, Oak Hill, makes you feel like you should be dressed in nineteenth century attire. Oak Hill was the childhood home of Miss Martha McChesney Berry, founder of Berry School, the forerunner of Berry College. The story of this school, founded in 1902, is told at the Museum. Other places on campus to see are the Old Mill, Possum Trot, The Ford Buildings, and the three Chapels. So dress casual and comfortable. Lunch will be on campus, also a gift shop and bookstore are open for browsing and buying.

Just north of Rome on Hwy 27 is The Martha Berry Museum and Art Galley. At the intersection of Hwy 27 and

81

Veterans Memorial Highway turn right and immediately turn right again into the entrance of Oak Hill, once the home of the Berry family. Follow the signs and the first stop is the Museum, which serves as a reception center for visitors. At the museum you can view a film about Miss Berry and the beginning of the school. Other memorabilia associated with the school are displayed here also. The museum also houses an excellent art collection given by a sister of Miss Berry. Near here is the small original log cabin (Circa 1872) where Miss Berry first taught the children from the mountain.

MARTHA BERRY MUSEUM AND ART GALLERY

A gift shop is located near the museum and has a picnic area, snacks and restrooms. A trail "Walkway of Life" leaves this area and winds through the scenic woods to Oak Hill. Refer to diagram to visit the gardens and green houses behind the plantation home. You may drive to Oak Hill but I suggest the walk if the weather is agreeable.

Martha McChesney Berry born in 1866 was the daughter of Captain Thomas Berry, a Civil War Veteran and Rome business man, and Frances Rhea Berry. Miss Berry had a vision; with her gift of inspiring others to help, she opened the school, which evolved into today's Berry College. She demanded labor from some, charmed speeches from the shy, drew praise from the cynical, and attracted major gifts from the Nation's leaders. Among them were Henry Ford, Andrew Carnegie, and many others. She devoted her life to the School and lived on the grounds or at Oak Hill until her death in 1942. Her portrait now hangs in Georgia's capital building and she is regarded as one of the most outstanding women in history

Martha McChesney Berry   1866 – 1942

OAK HILL – Berry Family Home

Oak Hill, the Berry family home, is a magnificent example of the classic Southern plantation home. Built in 1847 the home remains, as it was when Miss Berry lived there, a perfect backdrop for the gracious living enjoyed in the South by the more fortunate members of her generation. Surrounded by manicured lawns and giant aged oak trees, the grounds are beautifully maintained and provide a sense of serenity long to be remembered.

Student guides, who attend Berry College, will tell you the story of one of the most remarkable of America's daughters, Miss Martha Berry. In 1902 she started and taught a school for children who lived in the mountains. They were too far away for them to attend any other school. She would take her buggy with her horse 'Roanie' and bring the children to school here. Later it became a boarding school, where the students worked for their keep. They raised crops for food, raised cattle, and kept dairy cows. This taught them a work skill along with their classroom learning.

I visited the Carriage House near the home and heard the story of 'Roanie' the pony who served Miss Berry for thirty-four years. You can visit his grave on the main campus. Miss Berry's buggy, her Mother's surrey, and a 1914 Ford touring car are on display in the Carriage House, along with a 1917 model-T and the 1940 Mercury that was Miss Berry's personal car until the time of her death. Also a 1930 Ford tractor is seen here. You may hear the story of Henry Ford giving the school tractors to replace the mule teams.

The gardens of Oak Hill are its crowning glory, don't miss them. Walk through the formal gardens and nature trails, which were the pride of Miss Berry and of her Mother. The fountain in the first rectangular pool was cast in France. The beautiful cherry trees in the terrace garden were an official gift of the Japanese government. Also a most unique sunken garden is located in the garden area. You may visit the greenhouses by requesting the tour earlier.

OAK HILL & THE MARTHA BERRY MUSEUM GROUNDS

After entering from Veterans Hwy turn right to the Museum. Behind these building is the walking trail to Oakhill. The Coach house is first then the large home. The gardens are connected to the grounds and the greenhouse is past them. The exit is at lower right and enters Martha Berry Boulevard.

It's time to leave this quiet peaceful place and continue north on Hwy 27 for a short distance to the main entrance of Berry College. Turn right on Hwy 27 after existing the grounds, go to the second red light and turn left into the Campus. A map available from the Museum or at the gate is very helpful to find your way around this large campus.

This beautiful Campus is a place to explore the history of this interesting institution. Turn right at the first road off the circle and view the English Gothic structures of the Ford Complex. This consists of seven buildings forming a quadrangle around a serene reflection pool. The buildings are used as dormitories for women, classrooms, a gymnasium, and an auditorium. Funds for this complex were a gift from automobile magnate, Henry Ford in the 1920's. The Ford Foundation provided funds and in 2002 a complete remodeling and update of these historic buildings was completed. They now include an alumni center and multi purpose rooms for special events as well as the female dorm rooms, dining hall, auditorium, classrooms, and gym.

BARNWELL CHAPEL MOUNT BERRY, GEORGIA

Continue your drive past Barnwell Chapel. Berry is fortunate to have three historic chapels on its campus and all are wonderfully designed. Each is a favorite place for many weddings of the young people who have attended college here.

Barnwell Chapel, a log building, was designed and built in 1911 by Captain John Barnwell, a friend of Miss Berry.

FROST MEMORIAL CHAPEL

The Frost Memorial Chapel, which you will see on the Mountain Campus, was built from funds donated by Mr. and Mrs. Howard Frost in memory of their son.

The largest and most visible chapel on the campus is College Chapel; you will stop to visit it on your return from the Mountain Campus. This building commands the entire central campus area and was designed by Harry Carlson of Boston, Massachusetts, the same architect that designed the Ford Buildings. This chapel, completed in 1915 by students, was modeled after Christ Church in Alexandria, Virginia. It has been expanded to seat eleven hundred people. A set of chimes was presented to the chapel on October 7, 1941, Miss Berry's seventy-fifth birthday. She died a few months later. Her grave is located just south of the chapel where an eternal flame burns in her honor. Called the 'Shining Light Award', it was bestowed due to her efforts as one who blazed the trail of knowledge for others.

Back to our tour, after seeing the log cabin area of Guest Cottages, Nursery School, and Barnwell Chapel, head to the Mountain Campus three miles from there. After the scenic drive turn right and pause at Swan Lake to watch the graceful swans and geese. Continue around by Frost Chapel on the hill to your right and drive by other buildings in the area. They are home to some of the students of Berry College. Winshape Center is located here.

You are now at the foot of Lavender Mountain and going to see the Old Mill. Deer and other wildlife are seen any time of the year on this short drive. The Old Mill stands as one of the largest wooden overshot waterwheels in the world. Constructed in 1930 and used for many years to grind corn into meal. The wheel was rebuilt during 1985 and operates two times a year for visitors and Berry Alumni. In its wooded mountain setting, with a pond to reflect it and the stone building near by, it is one of the most photographed settings in North Georgia. So don't forget your camera and film.

On your return follow the map and drive by the Normandy Apartments and Dairy Barns. They were used until the 1980's for a dairy herd, which provided food for the College. Students work for part of their expenses and this was one area that provided jobs. Built in the 1930's, the building have been rebuilt for a different use, they will retain the French-style architecture. The new buildings have the same architect look as the barns. Camp Winshape, a camp for girls and the Rollins Center, an equestrian center update this part of the campus. The buildings, along with new ones house a lodge for overnight retreats, meeting and conference space complete with a café, a spa and dining hall.

Take a right turn and visit the mountain church built in 1850. The Possum Trot Church is sometimes called "the cradle of Berry College." Martha Berry began teaching Sunday School here in 1900. It was the needs of the mountain people she met here that inspired her to build her schools. She painted scriptures on the walls of the church, some of which can still be seen today. The church was used as a grammar school in the early 1930's. It officially closed as a classroom in 1954. Each year a homecoming is held to celebrate Possum Trot's significance to Berry College.

POSSUM TROT CHURCH

The first weekend in October is Mountain Day at Berry College. Alumni and students celebrate Miss Berry's birthday by gathering on the Mountain Campus for picnics and a march down the hill holding hands. They also give donations to commemorate her birthday.

Now return to the Main Campus and continue your tour of the South end of this beautiful campus. Stop at the College Chapel to view this striking church and to see Miss Berry's grave. Be sure to see the Roosevelt Cabin, built around 1902. Designed and built by Captain Barnwell soon after the schools opened, it was to be used as a guesthouse and social event center. Miss Berry even lived in this cabin for four years because she felt that living at Oak Hill would make her lazy. The cabin's namesake and most famous visitor was President Theodore Roosevelt who ate lunch here with Miss Berry on October 8, 1910. The former President Roosevelt visited Rome on that date.

The "House of Dreams" is located atop Lavender Mountain. This home for Miss Berry was built by the students in the 1930's. It has been preserved as it was when she lived there and is only open by special request.

Complete your tour by way of Krannert Center, near the entrance gate. This building has a cafeteria, bookstore, post office, and dining hall that is open to visitors during the college terms. You may lunch here.

Berry is history, beauty and tranquility; it is also an excellent school of higher learning. The College has been ranked, as reported in U.S. News and World Report, as one of the top liberal-arts colleges in the nation. Top ranked faculty and staff provide tremendous support to the student body. Persons from the fifty states and various foreign countries come here to study, work, and learn.   I hope you have enjoyed your visit here today. Please come again if there wasn't enough time to see everything.

After lunch, "Are you ready to move on to our next adventure?"   The next stop is just a short distance north on Highway 27, turn left after exiting the gate of the college.

You can make a choice between Stonebridge Golf Course and Mount Berry Square Mall. I'll tell you about the golf course first.

Located in the scenic Appalachian foothills of Georgia, Stonebridge Golf Club offers quality, affordability, and convenience.   It begins with an eighteen hole, par seventy-two championship layout that has Bermuda grass fairways winding among tall pines leading to challenging bentgrass greens. There is a modern clubhouse and pro shop, complete practice areas, shower and locker facilities, and a full service grill. Quality PGA instructions are offered.

It is located at 585 Stonebridge Drive.   One quarter mile past Berry College, turn left onto the Old Summerville Road, then follow the signs.   Those who don't play golf can visit the mall nearby.

The Mall area on the right side of Highway 27 has movie theaters, restaurants, play area, plenty of parking, and shopping. This 460,000 square foot mall has an indoor walking area as well as stores, shops, food, beauty salons, and more. You could spend a full day here with rest stops and lunch. The out parcels have fun for the younger ones and a nine screen movie theater.   More restaurants are nearby for you dinner.

If there is time left today or perhaps another day you must visit the Rocky Mountain Recreation and Public Fishing Area. It is located at 4054 Big Texas Valley Road. Continue North on

Highway 27 and turn left at Big Texas Valley Road. The Rocky Mountain project began in the 1970's and was built by Oglethorpe Power Corporation. This was a major undertaking to make electricity by water power in a different way. This project removed the top of a mountain and built a holding pond on top. Water is released to produce power, then pumped back to the top pond, when demand is low, to be used again to produce power as needed.

Rocky Mountain Recreation Area

This public area includes two recreation lakes totaling five hundred fifty nine acres. Largemouth bass and sunfish are the most common game fish species in both lakes, however channel catfish, black crappie, and hybrid white striped bass are also there.

White-tail deer, turkey, and waterfowl frequent the area proving visitors an opportunity to observe wildlife in a natural setting. The lakes, with a backdrop of forested ridgelines, offer visitors a scenic and relaxed setting. You can enjoy fishing, hunting, picnicking, hiking, camping, and swimming. A Georgia fishing license is required. Wildlife Management Area stamp not required. Other regulations are posted at the site. A parking fee must be paid when you enter.

Rocky Mountain Recreation Area is open year-round, sunrise to sunset, seven days a week. Fishing is permitted from sunrise to sunset, seven days a week. Camping season is April 1st through October 31st. The group picnic shelter is available by reservation only. Picnic shelters and restrooms are provided. Maybe you should come prepared for an evening cookout and marshmallow roast,

Chapter VII

Day VII

PRAISE TIME - RIVERS THREE

"Give unto the Lord the glory due unto his name; Worship the Lord in the beauty of holiness"

Psalm 29:2

I suggest his day be a Sunday. Our plan is for you to visit a different church. Remember you are on vacation, so your church isn't expecting you today. Included are synopses and history of eight beautiful historic churches in downtown Rome. Choose one of these to attend this morning. Refer to the downtown map in Chapter One to find the church you decide to attend. Then we will have lunch and tour more parks, rivers, and the Library.

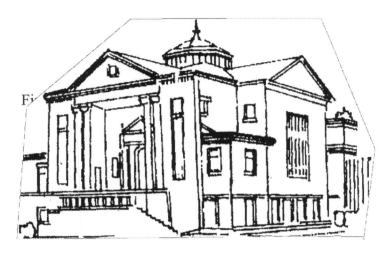

First Christian Church, Disciples of Christ - 209 Second Avenue was first organized in the home of Mrs. G. Cross, with twelve charter members. The architecture of the church is known as the standard or Akron plan and similar churches are to be found in Athens and Griffin, Georgia. The Rome church is built of Georgia marble and is the only marble church building among the Christian Churches in Georgia. The marble was a gift from Mr. Sam Tate, Sr. of Tate, Georgia and the North Carolinas. The St. Louis Railroad transported the marble blocks from Tate to Rome free of charge. Mr. Bill Gunn was the very capable stone mason who supervised the laying of the marble. The stained glass windows are particularly lovely and in the center of the sanctuary there is a skylight dome with panels of stained glass.

First United Methodist Church

The Rome First United Methodist Church, now located at 202 East Third Street, has had three homes. The first was a log school building on Eight Avenue; the second was a wooden structure built in 1840 on the corner of East Second Street and Sixth Avenue. This was later replaced by a brick building. In 1880 the present lot was purchased and the current building built with the opening service in 1888. This present church is of Gothic Romanesque design built of handmade pink brick. On the inside of the church on the left wall there is a marble plaque with the names of the six ladies who organized the church in 1840. The sanctuary is paneled in oak with a sculptured wooden ceiling. Adding to the beauty of the interior of the church are stained glass windows and handmade wooden flower pedestals and baptismal font. An administration building was added to the original church in 1941 and an educational building in 1964. Other expansions took place in the mid-1990's. The fountain and wind-bells in the central courtyard have Christian symbols and were make by Karl Dance, a Rome resident and talented ironwork designer.

First Presbyterian Church

The First Presbyterian Church at 101 East Third Avenue was organized in 1833 at Livingston, Georgia. The church was later transferred to Rome in 1845. The present church was dedicated in 1849. The present sanctuary dates from 1854. The bricks used in the construction were made on the Bailey Farm on the Coosa River a short distance from Rome. In 1864 the building was taken over by the Union Army and used for food storage. The Rev. S.E. Axson, D.D. served as leader from 1866 until 1883, covering an important period of history. One of his daughters, Ellen Louise, became the beloved wife of Woodrow Wilson, who later became the 28th President of the United States. A Reuter organ is in the sanctuary and was given in memory of Kathryn Henley Wyatt.

First Baptist Church

First Baptist Church, 100 East Fourth Avenue, was organized in 1835 the same year that Rome received its charter from the state. The first building was at the corner of Eighth Avenue and West

First Street. The present site was purchased in 1855 and a brick church building was erected. That building was replaced in 1883 by a larger brick building that served this congregation for over one hundred years. When the Union Army occupied Rome in 1864, they removed the pews from the church to help make pontoon bridges over the rivers. Horses were quartered in part of the basement. This congregation was a co-founder of the Cherokee Baptist Female College in 1873 (now Shorter College). The pastor of the church, Rev. Luther Gwaltney, and one of its leading members, Col. Alfred Shorter, provided the idea and the money for the new school.

Saint Peter's Episcopal Church

Saint Peter's Episcopal Church at 101 East Fourth Avenue was organized in March 1844 when Rome was ten years old. In 1853 the congregation was able to erect a suitable building. During the war the church carpet was removed and given for use as blankets for Confederate soldiers. During the Federal Occupation of

Rome in 1864, both the church and adjoining rectory were used as a hospital by occupying Union forces. On Christmas Day 1898, the first Holy Communion was celebrated in the present church building. By 1914 the memorial stained glass windows and all its principal furnishings were installed in the church.

The Rodeph Sholom Congregation (Pursuers of Peace) was formed as a congregation in 1871. The first services were held in the Masonic Temple Annex. In 1938, Rodelph Sholom Congregation dedicated the new synagogue located at 406 East First Street. A central lighting fixture in the synagogue is unique. This handsome chandelier came from a cathedral in Brussels and originally held candles. From the turn of the century until 1955 the Hebrew Union College of Cincinnati sent a student rabbi to Rome to serve during the High Holy Days and for twice a month weekend visits. For several years, an ordained Rabbi from Atlanta has led the congregation, conducts Friday evening services, and serves other needs of the congregation. (No Sketch)

The Saint Paul AME Church, which stands at 106 East Sixth Avenue, was built in 1840. The first wooden structure was built on a corner lot donated by Colonel D. R. Mitchell with a stipulation in the deed that the property would always be used for a church building. The frame building was replaced by a brick building in 1852 and used as the Methodist Church of Rome. During the Civil War all furniture was removed from the church building and the room in the basement was used to stable horses belonging to the Federal Army. In 1884 the building was sold to the AME Church. (No Sketch)

Metropolitan United Methodist Church

The Metropolitan United Methodist Church, corner of Broad Street and Seventh Avenue, was organized in October 1867, and is one of the oldest churches of the former Georgia conference. The first building occupied by the congregation was an attractive white frame structure topped with a graceful steeple. It is said to have been one of Rome's oldest buildings, having been erected prior to such landmarks as the City Clock Tower and the Old County Courthouse. It was on the same site as the present structure but faced the Seventh Avenue side of the site. The cornerstone for the present structure, which replaced the first building, was laid in 1910. Its sturdy brick construction, the spacious sanctuary, the beautifully designed stained glass windows (each one being given by members of the congregation), the custom built walnut pews, pulpit and alter chairs are evidence of the foresight, love, and Christian dedication of its early members

Saint Mary's Catholic Church

Saint Mary's Catholic Church is located at 911 North Broad Street. The first Catholic Church in Rome named St. Mary's was built in 1874. It was a simple frame building on Court Street which is now East First Street. It served the Catholic community until 1930 when the present building was constructed. Designed by a Benedictine Monk from Belmont Abbey in North Carolina, this church reflects the simplicity of monastic architecture and the spirit of the early Gothic period. Built of Stone Mountain granite and gracefully proportioned, it presents a compelling façade of the crucifixion in carved limestone, which forms the structure of the window in the choir loft. The stained glass in the lower windows is exceptionally detailed and reflects a European style and artistry. A large painting in the East transept is noteworthy. It is a copy of a masterpiece by Correggio, done by one of his students between 1518 and 1534. It was given by Princess Ruspoli,, the former Jennie Berry of Rome, sister of Martha Berry. In 1999 an extensive building program added another area to the building and updated the gardens.

After services, proceed to Broad Street and Second Avenue for brunch or lunch. The three story building on the West Side of Broad Street was built in the late 1800's and served as a bank for many, many years. Little remains of the bank but if look carefully you can still see the large safe.

It is now Magretta Hall, a special occasion restaurant. Beautifully and tastefully decorated with tremendous brass chandeliers, and graceful tall windows. Soft background music adds to the serene atmosphere. Pay particular attention to the painting of "Magretta", a lovely lady of English nobility, her home on the river at Rome was the original Magretta Hall. Lunch is a special occasion here every Sunday and lunch is also served at noon on Tuesday open to the public. Enjoy the food and music but don't stay too long because there's more to see in historic downtown.

The Oostanaula River and Old Floyd County Courthouse

"Time Marches on, still we can see.

The lovely, flowing rivers three."

Orlena Mitchell Warner

After lunch it's time to change into your walking shoes. Head toward the rivers, all three are less than a block away. Go south on Broad Street one block and turn right. You will see the lighted Robert Redden foot bridge across the Oostanaula. Mr.

Robert Redden was a local artist, well know for his pen and ink drawings of the landmarks of Rome and surrounding area. As you walk over the former railway bridge, view the meeting of the Etowah and Oostanaula rivers flowing together to form the Coosa River. Imagine a 170-foot steamboat as it might have come up the Coosa River to Rome in 1836. Riverboats of later years included the "Hill City", 140 by 18-feet, built in 1882 at Gadsen, Alabama; the "Sidney P. Smith" named for a local doctor, measured 139 by 24-feet and operated until 1884; the "John J. Seary" measured 172 by 28- feet; and "The Alabama" that could carry up to 200 people. These boats carried cargo and passengers from Gadsen and Chattanooga to Rome. There were many riverboats still in use at the turn of the twentieth century. Outings on riverboats were a favorite group activity. Large hunting parties chartered these wood-burning boats. People from the Cherokee Indians to the present day visitors and residents have always enjoyed fishing and hunting on the rivers.

Next you enter Heritage Park, built to commemorate the Nation's bicentennial in 1976. The park features bicycle and walking paths, picnic facilities, and a boat ramp. This park also has ball fields used by all ages. Some of your group may chose to bicycle or go boating this afternoon, instead of our planned walk.

Rest a bit under the gazebo and get ready for your river walk. This is a walk by the river not on the water. The paved path leads under the Robert Redden footbridge and under the Second Avenue Bridge and along the West Side of the Oostanaula River. On the opposite bank of the river you will see the Forum and the Floyd County Government building setting along side the Old Floyd County Courthouse. The Forum is a Civic Center complex located on the East bank of the river in the heart of Historic Downtown Rome. The connected building is The judicial center where court is held for Floyd County and joins the Forum by an overhead walkway. An outdoor plaza is located between the two large buildings. Memorial plaques located in the plaza list the names of Floyd County people who lost their lives in war. The Forum, with its meeting rooms, exhibition hall, and arena space, seats over four thousand people. The Forum has food and beverage services available. This is a great place for everything from conventions to seminars, receptions, and concerts.

THE FORUM

Next we cross the river at the Fifth Avenue Bridge and walk pass the huge Rome-Floyd Law Enforcement building and parking deck. The Statue on the front lawn is in memory of those who have died defending the laws of our county. Continue your walk North on West First Street for two blocks and you will see our beautiful library.

The Rome Floyd County Library

Our destination is the Rome-Floyd County Library located on the East Side of the river at 205 Riverside Parkway. The Rome-Floyd County Library is headquarters for the Sara Hightower Regional Library system which serves all of Floyd and Polk counties. This building dedicated in 1988, sits on the bank of the Oostanaula River and is an interesting, rewarding, and educational attraction. The unusual blend of tradition and contemporary architecture allows it to blend with the downtown district. Located on seven and one-half acres this 75,000-sq. ft. building can house 500,000 books. Other than books and reading material, you will find a vast selection of video films and audio books. The library also includes meeting space for up to 350 people, a computer center, a children's theatre, a literacy center, a talking book library for the handicapped, a production center for cable TV broadcasts, and a history room for genealogy research. Genealogy enthusiasts could spend days in the history room. A glass enclosed children's section was designed to allow the children to be themselves while adults have peace and quiet. The library is truly "a lighthouse for those who seek wisdom" and a dream come true for the people of Floyd County. Enjoy your visit here but not for long.

After you leave the library, well rested we hope, continue along the riverwalk on the North side of the Oostanula to Ridge Ferry Park. The trail leaves from the library parking lot. Or if you are not up to more walking, jog the next leg of our tour, call a taxi, or ask a friendly Roman to return you to get your car. It's less than a mile by the river walk or drive on Riverside Parkway approximately one mile. Ridge Ferry Park, named for Major Ridge a Cherokee who lived near here, is a fifty-four acre site and includes walking and jogging paths along the river. The wetlands area of the park with wood walkways allows students and visitors to view the plants and life found growing in the water. Also available for your enjoyment are picnic and playground facilities, bathrooms, covered pavilions, and canoe and kayak access. The "Roman Holiday" is moored here. It is a 55-passenger boat, owned by the City of Rome and can be rented by the day or for an evening and comes with a Captain. A group picnic or fishing cruise is a great way to entertain visitors. Sit for a spell and enjoy the relaxed atmosphere here.

State Mutual Baseball Stadium is just around the curve at the intersection of Riverside Parkway and Veterans Memorial By-Pass. It was built in 2002-2003 with funds from a tax voted in by the people of Floyd County. It was ready for the Rome Braves, a Class A minor league club, to begin an award winning season in April 2003. We hope you can attend a baseball game here.

State Mutual Baseball Stadium

Next we travel back along Riverside Parkway (maybe someone has retrieved your transportation), pause to visit the duck pond on the left. Feed the ducks and notice the Welcome Center on Jackson Hill. I doubt there is time to visit Jackson Hill and Fort Norton today. We'll visit them another day. Just across Turner McCall Boulevard you will find restaurants for you evening meal.

Elizabeth Oliver Wooten

CHAPTER VIII

DAY VIII

PARKS – BARNSLEY GARDENS

Happiness resides not in possession,
And not in gold.
The feeling of happiness
Dwells in the soul.
Democritus

Today is the extra, or alternate day, of our week of fun at home. Provided you have skipped one or have an extra day of vacation, you might want to include these activities. It really is a choice you will have to make. You may rest or explore the parks, tennis courts, ball fields, or other museums and attractions that we have not visited. Rome and Floyd County and surrounding area have lots of these. I'll tell you about some of them and others are listed in Chapter Ten.

If one day of your vacation is a non sunshine day, head for the library. The Rome/Floyd County Library on Riverside Drive has much to offer. Great books; books on tape or CD; movies; music on record, tape, or CD and video; and the History Room offers research on your family or other events. Check out your favorite, take it home, find a comfortable place and enjoy the day. Don't let friends or family know you are home.

If you are not a sports person may I suggest a day to be pampered. We have day spas, beauty shops, and massage therapist that will please any person. Make an appointment, have your hair colored, cut and styled, get a manicure and pedicure, a facial and massage, and enjoy all of it. It may be a bit expensive but so is golf, or a trip and all that goes with that type of vacations.

A walk in the woods is an excellent morale booster for anyone. Especially if those woods are landscaped and well cared for. The Rome-Floyd area has 800 acres of developed park and recreation land. There are two regional parks, ten community parks, nine neighborhood parks and other specialized facilities. Walking and jogging trails are found in many of these. Heritage park, near downtown Rome, at the confluence of the rivers begins the Rails-to-Trails walking trail. This path follows the abandoned railroad right-of-way and continues along the Etowah River for many miles. Another Rails-to-Trail conversion is the Simms Mountain Trail, which is the first leg of the Pinhoti Trail in the state of Georgia. This trail will connect to the existing Pinhoti Trail in Alabama. These parks and outdoor activities will allow you to enjoy the beautiful natural scenery of this area. Discover nature and beauty along these scenic trails by foot, boat, horse, skates, or bicycle. A brochure with map is available at the Visitors Center.

If jogging and walking aren't for you how about sports activities? There are more than thirty game level sports fields and more practice level sports areas. Organized ball teams and competition are always available through the Rome-Floyd Parks and Recreation Authority. Their office is at 300 W. Third Street in Rome. The Rome YMCA and Boys and Girls Club offer many activities for the youth.

The tennis courts offer excellent facilities for the tennis player. Many state and area tennis tournaments are held here. Try these for an enjoyable day of healthful outdoor activity. If the weather is hot you may enjoy the swimming pool. The other facilities include a Gymnastics Center, Fitness Center, Stadium Track, Nature Center, Skate Center, Farmers Market, Greenways and Trails, RV Campground, and a Golf Driving Range.

Walking trails along the river between our two downtown parks are excellent for those who are not in shape for much physical activity. You can begin in Heritage Park and go north along the Oostanaula River, cross over the River and follow the trail near the River to Ridge Ferry Park. Continue and you will be at the Chieftain's Museum. Or better yet - State Mutual Baseball Stadium is a little farther out at Riverside Pkwy and Veterans Memorial By-Pass. Maybe the Rome Braves will have a home game today or at least go see the Stadium and visit their gift shop.

Besides the public parks and programs, Rome is home to three movie complexes with nineteen screens, two malls, many restaurants, and unique shops downtown. The Rome Symphony is the oldest organized symphony in Georgia and is a very active part of the cultural arts of this area. The Rome Little Theater provides excellent community plays by local people. Berry and Shorter College art departments also have many programs you are invited to attend. Programs by the Rome Area Council on the Arts, include shows by local artist and artisans.

If it's summer and baseball season you have another treat for this extra day you have. The Rome Braves began there first season in Rome in 2003. This team won the Championship in their division in 2003. State Mutual Stadium is very people friendly and small enough to see everything. The facilities are well-planned and easy to enter, even for the handicapped. The store is well stocked with Rome Braves items and food is available throughout the area.

Special events that are held annually are, Floyd County Fair and Carnival, Heritage Holidays, which includes a Wagon Trail

115

Ride and Parade downtown, and the Chiaha Festival all held in October. Mayfest is a spring celebration. First Friday Concerts are held downtown from May through October. They are free events preformed outside if the weather allows. See the listing in Chapter Ten for other programs.

Chieftains Museum, Clock Tower Museum, Rome Area History Museum, Eubanks Gallery, Oak Hill and Martha Berry Museum, and Rome Area History Museum are all located in the Rome and Floyd County area. Shorter, Berry, and Floyd Colleges, and Coosa Valley Technical School are here also. They have classes for all ages, check on what you are interested in. These and other attractions are listed in Chapter Ten. We hope you can visit all of these interesting places someday.

If you would like a short day trip I suggest Barnsley Gardens. This attraction is located at 595 Barnsley Gardens Road, eight miles southwest of Adairsville GA. snd about twelve miles from Rome. This attraction has a very interesting history. The story begins in the 1830's. Godfrey Barnsley, a young wealthy Cotton Merchant, visited the area around Adairsville. He felt this climate was better than Savannah, GA., for his family of a young wife and five children. He purchased about ten thousand acres of land in Northwest Georgia and began plans for a twenty-six room, three story home. He decided to have it built on a hill reputedly shunned by Indians who warned him to choose a different site. Construction started in 1844 on the Italian villa, called Woodlands. Barnsley, who was opposed to slavery, wanted most of his brick-making and other building work contracted to others in the area. Tiles for the floor were imported, doors and paneling were make in England, mantels of marble were brought from Italy.

The family lived in a cabin during the summer months while construction began on their new home, ignoring warnings by Cherokee Indians who insisted that the place was unlucky and misfortune would come. Before the work was completed Julia Barnsley was stricken with a disease and died in 1845. Her husband and the children planned to carry on the building in her memory. In 1850 the oldest Barnsley daughter, Anna, married and moved to New Orleans. The second daughter, Adelaide came home to Woodlands in 1857 and died shortly after.

Godfrey Barnsley was now obsessed with completing the mansion. He toured Europe and purchased elegant furnishings and art treasures including a Louis XVI bed, mahogany dining room pieces, Venetian mirrors, and a five-hundred piece china setting that bore a motif from his coat of arms. His oldest son, Howard, was killed by pirates in 1862 while in China helping to buy plants for his father's gardens.

The Civil War interrupted the plans to complete the home in memory of Julia. Barnsley was past the age for military service in 1863 but sent his two remaining sons, George and Lucian, to fight for the Confederacy. His daughter Julia married a Confederate Caption James P. Baltzelle, who sent Julia to Savannah for safety.

Federal Troops, found Godfrey alone in his unfinished house, which only needed parquet flooring and a carved master staircase to be complete. These never arrived due to the War. His presence did not stop the looting of his treasures. Furnishing were destroyed, Italian statuary was smashed, windows and china were broken. Food and everything that they could they took with.

George and Lucian Barnsley returned after the war, but refused to sign the oath of allegiance to forces they had just fought against. They left the county with other Confederate veterans, and settled in Sao Paulo, Brazil. They never came back to live at the

Woodlands. Godfrey Barnsley died at New Orleans in 1873. His body was returned and buried at Woodlands.

Julia, Barnsley's daughter, had one daughter Adelaide, born in 1864. Adelaide's father Baltzelle was killed in 1864 and Julia remarried. She later returned to live at Woodlands. Adelaide, died young, leaving two small sons. One of her sons killed his brother and was sent to prison. After their deaths, Woodlands and the estate was sold at auction. It seems the Indian's predictions of bad luck did come to this family.

The old building, in bad condition, still stands and is part of the tourist attraction today. You will see the remains of the home that was never really finished. The gardens were the showplace of estate and today have been restored to part of their former beauty. They were said to have covered twenty acres along the drive to the villa.

Enjoy your day, whether you do one of these things or simply rest.

Remember 'Happiness ... dwells in the soul'.

CHAPTER IX

IT'S FUN TO ENTERTAIN

A pleasant and happy life does not come from external things – Man draws from within himself, as from a spring, pleasure and joy.   *Plutarch*

Now that you have had a relaxing vacation with no hassle it's time to entertain your friends or family. I'll include some ideas and suggestions to get you started. One is for a dinner at home with a few friends, another is a cookout at home or in a park depending on how many you invite, and then suggestions of fun at a family reunion or group party. Some menus and the recipes included are guaranteed to be excellent dishes.

Please understand, I am not a great cook, it must be easy and quick if I do it. I taught my daughters that the best thing you can make for dinner are reservations at the best restaurant in town.

Let's begin with the dinner party. If this is more than you want to do, take a look at the Hobo Dinner one.

The Dinner Party Menu

Chicken Roll-Ups in Mushroom Gravy

Honey Carrots - Rice

Tiny Green Pea Salad

Berries in Sherry Cream

Bran Rolls

Water   Tea   Coffee

RECIPES

Chicken Roll-Ups in Mushroom Sauce

6 boneless chicken breasts   1 jar dried beef slices
6 slices bacon (half strips may be used or partially
precook bacon and discard fat)
1 (4 oz.) carton sour cream
1 can cream of mushroom soup
2 tablespoons cooking sherry.

Flatten chicken breasts, put 2 slices of dried beef on each breast and roll up. Put a slice of bacon around each roll and fasten with a toothpick. Use any leftover beef in bottom of baking dish. Mix next three ingredients together and pour over chicken roll-ups. Bake 45 minutes at 375 degrees. Serve with rice.

Honey Carrots

1 pound of carrots
4 tablespoons honey
4 tablespoons butter
½ tsp. salt
Dried parsley flakes

Peel carrots, leave whole, place on a large piece of heavy foil. Drizzle honey over carrots, put pats of butter on this, and sprinkle salt and parsley flakes on top. Fold foil to seal, place on baking dish and bake at 350 degrees for 1 hour.

Tiny Green Pea Salad

1 (17 oz.) can petite garden peas (frozen peas can be   used.)
1 (4 oz.) jar diced pimiento
1 c. grated Cheddar cheese
½ c. finely chopped celery
1 small onion, finely chopped
1 (2 oz.) package slivered almonds
2 Tblsp. Mayonnaise
Lettuce leaves

Drain peas and pimientos. In medium bowl, combine next four   ingredients with peas and pimientos. Toss with dressing. Cover and chill at least one hour. Serve on lettuce leaves.

Berries in Sherry Sauce

1 qt. Raspberries, fresh or frozen (strawberries or blackberries may be substituted)
1 c. whipping cream
2 lg. Eggs
2 T. sugar
2 T. sherry
½ t. almond extract
Pinch of salt

Wash berries, if fresh, and chill. If frozen, defrost and set aside to stay chilled. Heat cream in top of double boiler. Separate eggs. Beat yolks with sugar until smooth. Pour small amounts of hot cream into yolks, beating constantly to avoid lumping. Continue cooking till mixture thickens. Add sherry, almond extract and salt to cream sauce. Beat egg whites until stiff and fold into cool sauce. When ready to serve, spoon chilled berries into individual serving dishes and top with cream sauce. Cream sauce may be prepared ahead and served cold.

Bran Rolls

1 cup boiling water
1 cup shortening
1 c. All Bran Cereal
2/3 cup sugar
2 eggs, well beaten
2 pkg. yeast, dissolved in 1 cup lukewarm water
6 to 8 cups self-rising flour.

Pour boiling water over shortening and cereal Cool to lukewarm and add sugar, beaten eggs and yeast cakes dissolved in lukewarm water. Stir in flour by cupfuls. Dough will be sticky. Cover bowl and keep in warm place two hours or refrigerate overnight. Make into rolls and let rise two hours in warm place. Use melted butter for bowl and top of dough and on hands to prevent sticking. This dough may be kept in refrigerator several days. Bake in 375-degree oven for 25 minutes. Makes about 50 rolls.

The recipes all serve eight to ten people if doubled. You may want to try them for your family and decide how many you want to invite. Plan your shopping list and guest list and call a friend to help if you are about to panic. Everything is easier with a friend by your side.

I believe all parties should have a theme. This menu is best for a small group of six to twelve. This allows you to use your dining room and good china if you wish. It could be a birthday or anniversary celebration, a romantic dinner for two; (all of the dishes can be prepared ahead of time), leaving time to prepare yourself. Don't forget the candlelight.

After selecting the theme or event, next are invitations. After date, time, place, etc. include one line about the party to indicate the theme and dress. (It's Mom's birthday, she still believes in dressing for dinner.) A response from each guest is needed any time you are serving food. Even after responding some people will forget or fail to show. The day before call each guest (as a reminder) and ask, "Did I give you the time to arrive for our dinner tomorrow?" Or ask some similar question. This will assure you of how many to prepare for.

Set the table the day before. This allows more time to consider how you will serve, where to sit each guest and what exactly you will need. Serving buffet style works best for most meals, unless it is a formal dinner party. If it is formal find someone to serve the table. After all you have prepared everything and deserve to sit with you quests and enjoy the meal. A less formal affair allows everyone to serve themselves and they are more relaxed.

Place cards or a name at each place relieves the guest of having to decide where and with whom to sit. Try to find an interesting way to mix the people. By their birth month, by where they live, by the age of their children, etc. are some suggestions.

Names can be attached to their glass, tied around or on stem. This helps the server and they can find their glass all evening. The name can be placed on a small package, as their take home favor. It's fun and interesting to see the different small inexpensive favors you can find that fits each guest. A small vase and one flower at each place with name, (a rose for Rosemary, a daisy for Daisy) or all the same flower. These could also double as your table decoration. Please make your table decoration low enough to see the others at the table or it will be moved, usually by the husband. Items other than flowers can be used for decorating the table. They can help carry out your theme.

Most of this menu can be prepared earlier. Begin by making the yeast dough for the rolls the day before. This can be kept in the refrigerator for several days. After being made into rolls and left near the warm oven to rise they will be ready for baking just in time to serve. The carrots can be peeled any time and put in foil with seasoning ready to bake. Pea salad keeps well in the refrigerator. Chicken rollups can be prepared well in advance – ready to go in the oven along with the carrots. Allow time to bake the rolls after the rollups and carrots are done, unless you have two ovens. Now all that's left is preparing the dessert, according to the recipe, and fixing the drinks. .

ENJOY! I'm sure your guest will and think of the fun that you will have being entertained by them.

The next suggestion is a delicious meal that's easy to prepare and serve. This is a summertime outdoor party. Use colorful plastic tablecloths and paper plates and napkins to carry out your theme.

Large plastic cups with names written on them are perfect for place cards. Real silverware will be appreciated if you have enough for everyone.

MENU

Hobo Dinners with Vegetables
Baked Beans
Cole Slaw
Hard Rolls
Iced Tea or Canned Drinks
Homemade Ice Cream or
Apple Pie with Ice Cream

Hobo dinners are ground chuck – potatoes, carrots, onions, or other veggies, red and green peppers add color, - with seasonings. These are cut in small strips. The meat is made into oval patties about an inch thick, use about 1/3 pound per serving. Tear two strips of thick foil for each dinner. Place the meat and enough veggies for a serving on a piece of foil, add salt and pepper to taste. Fold the foil edges together and bi-fold again, and press down leaving a little air space, sealing all edges. Now place on the other sheet of foil and fold and seal it. These will be cooked on the grill for fifteen minutes, then turned and cooked fifteen minutes on the other side. After removing the outer foil they are ready to serve by slitting down the smooth side. Sometime I leave them in the foil and let the guest open and eat from the packet, or they can be dumped on the plate. I think we all have easy ways to prepare baked beans and cole slaw. Cabbage can be be purchased cut and ready to season. Canned beans just need a little brown sugar, catsup, mustard, Bar-B-Que sauce, and chopped onion added and cooked a short time.

I'll give you my easy recipe for fruit cobbler. Or a frozen pie, from the grocery store, with ice cream is a good dessert for this meal.

Southern Peach Cobbler

One large can sliced freestone peaches or 3 cups fresh peaches sweetened to taste. (I have used apples, blackberries, or blueberries, instead of peaches.) Add one cup of sugar to most fruits.

One stick butter
One cup sugar
One cup self-rising flour
One cup buttermilk. (One-teaspoon vinegar added to milk will substitute for buttermilk.)

Melt butter in an 8" by 12"casserole dish, while oven is preheating to 400 degrees. Heat the fruit with sugar in boiler on stove; next pour fruit into dish with the butter. Mix together sugar, flour, milk, and pour over fruit and melted butter. Shake dish to bring flour mixture to top of fruit. Bake 25 minutes or until lightly brown on top. Serve hot with ice cream. Makes 8 servings.

Now for the fun! If you don't have a pool for a swim event, just ask someone to plan old-fashioned outdoor games. Hop Scotch, Red Rover Come Over, Sack Races, Horseshoes, Egg Toss, or Balloon Toss give a variety for all ages. Begin with water filled balloons or raw egg toss. Let the children select an adult as their partner. The people make two lines facing their partner, near enough to touch their partner. Give a water filled balloon or raw egg to one of the partners (each couple has only one), they toss to their partner and then all step backwards and toss again. They usually are far apart before the balloon or egg is broken, to shower them and others. This gets all involved to start the fun filled evening. Next make suggestions for others events or set up a play off type tournament for the Horseshoes, Volley Ball, or an any game. People will form their own teams to make this fun. Don't forget the prizes for all winners.

We all need new recipes for the famous covered-dish meal we are invited too. One recipe that I must share comes from my husband's sister. One lady told me that she wasn't a good cook and hated to go to these events, but after sharing this dish one time she is now happy to go. She always takes this Corn and Green Bean Casserole and people love it.

Corn and Green Bean Casserole

2 (16 oz.) can French cut green beans
1 (12 oz.) can shoe peg corn
1 can celery soup
1 cup sour cream
½ cup grated mild Cheddar cheese
½ cup finely chopped onion
½ t. salt
½ cup butter or margarine
1 roll Ritz Crackers, crushed

Drain beans and corn, mix. Place in 9" by 12" casserole dish. Mix soup, sour cream, cheese, onion, and salt. Spread mixture over drained beans and corn. Melt butter in skillet on top of stove and mix with cracker crumbs. Spread over mixture. Bake uncovered at 350 degrees for 45 minutes.

I'm sure most of you have your favorite foods to share but this one is worth the effort to make. This recipe won first prize for a vegetable dish.

I'll give you one great idea for getting people acquainted with each other. I have used it at reunions and other gatherings. It is a great way to learn and remember people's names and learn something else about them. Those cousins at family reunions don't always mix well without encouragement. This gives them a reason to ask questions and not be embarrassed about not remembering their names.

These questions were prepared for a Christmas party. The questions can change depending on who the people are and what event they are attending. Copy this to a full sheet of paper with lines for the signature. Make a copy for each person and provide pens or pencils for everyone.

FIND SOMEONE WHO? (Get signatures from different people who the fit sentence. The person with the most DIFFERENT signatures that are true, (we will check the authenticity) wins the prize.

1. Who has served in the military? _____
2. Who has taught school? _____
3. Who has played football? _____
4. Who is wearing a red undergarment? _____

5. Who is or was a cheerleader? _____
6. Who was born after 1990? _____
7. Who has on green earrings? _____
8. Who traveled the most miles to get here? _____
9. Who arrived here first today? _____
10. Who was born before 1925? _____
11. Who has the most descendants? _____
12. Who has on two socks of different colors? _____
13. Who has green eyes? _____
14. Who has kicked her husband today? _____
15. Who has kissed his wife today?_____
16. Who has 32 teeth? _____
17. Who has six grand children? _____
18. Who has played Santa Claus? _____

Don't be afraid that people won't play, most of them will and my friends have always enjoyed this. Be prepared with two gifts in case of a tie. Bags of candy, can of nuts, or any food item is a good gift for the winner.

Here's another idea for a family reunion. Buy white or light colored apron or a tote bag in duck fabric. Get several different colors of permanent ink markers. Assign a teenager or two to get signatures from each person present in the color specified for their generation. For instance the oldest generation, the great great grandparents could sign in blue, next oldest generation, red etc. Or each color could represent a family group. Be sure to attach or write on the item the explanation of the colors used and the current date and place. These can be given to the oldest person or they become an auction item to help pay for the expense.

I hope you agree with me that it can be fun to entertain. Enjoy your family and friends today, don't wait – Life has an expiration date!

CHAPTER   X

GUIDE TO ATTRACTIONS

Museums

Chieftains Museum – A National Landmark located on the banks of the Oostanaula River that once served as the home of Major Ridge, a leader of the Cherokee Nation. The museum depicts the heritage of the house with a prevailing emphasis on the story of the Ridge family and the impact that they had on both Cherokee and American History. Located at 501 Riverside Pkwy, Rome, GA. For more information call 706 291-9494

City Clock Tower Museum – Four-sided clock located on one of the Seven Hills of Rome. It was built to provide water and fire protection. A Museum is located on the inside of the tank. The clock tower is the official symbol of the city of Rome. It is located near the intersection of East Fifth Ave. and East Second St. Call 706 295-5576 for more information.

Eubanks Gallery – Located just inside the entrance to Shorter College in the J. Robert Eubanks Welcome Center, the gallery has exhibits collected from the Eurbanks world travels, including African and Indian safaris. An Indian honey bear and African lion are among the prized trophy animals exhibited. Visitors will also discover an extensive array of early American tools, household and personal items as well as a collection of Native American artifacts. Gallery hours are 8:30 am to 5 PM M-F. For more information, call 706 233-7319

Historic Floyd County Courthouse– View the Beautiful woodwork in the courtroom as well as an eternal flame that pays tribute to veterans. The Courthouse was built in 1892 and is located on North Fifth Avenue near the Oostanula River.

Oak Hill & The Martha Berry Museum – A plantation house, museum and beautiful gardens are located on the former property of Martha Berry, founder of Berry College. The museum includes various exhibits describing the history of Berry College and Martha Berry. For more information call 706 291-1883.

Rome Area History Museum – Fascinating stories of adventure, exploration, and dedication await you at the Rome Area History Museum. You don't need the movies, come learn real stories of discovery and achievement. From Hernando DeSoto's visit to the are in 1540 to Civil War heroes, early physicians, barnstormers and beyond. This museum has a lot to show you about how Rome came to be what it is today. Located at 305 Broad Street, Rome. For more information call 706 235-8051.

Tellus Science Museum – 100 Tellus Drive, Cartersville, GA
www.tellusmuseum.org

Etowah Indian Mounds, 813 Indian Mounds Rd. S.W. Cartersville, GA.   770 387-3747

Booth Western Art Museum - 116 North Gilmer Street - Cartersville, GA   770 387-1300

Bartow History Center - 13 N. Wall Street Cartersville, GA

Chief Vann House - Chatsworth, GA. - Tuesday - Saturday 9 AM - 5 PM Sunday 2 - 5 PM 706 695-2598

LANDMARKS AND MONUMENTS

Capitoline Wolf Sculpture – Sculpture of Romulus and Remus was a gift to Rome, Georgia from Mussolini, in Rome, Italy. It is located in from of City Hall at 601 Broad Street.

Myrtle Hill Cemetery - Listed on the National Register of Historic Places, this cemetery includes Tomb of the Known Soldier, Ellen Axson Wilson's grave and Civil War Statues. It is located at South Broad just across the Coosa River.

Tomb of the Known Soldier – In honor of the 'known' soldiers from World War I. Located in Myrtle Hill Cemetery.

Ellen Axson Wilson Grave Site – Burial place for the first wife of President Woodrow Wilson. It is located in Myrtle Hill cemetery.

Civil War Statues – Honors the over 350 Civil War soldiers who died in battles near Rome, Georgia. Located in Myrtle Hill Cemetery.

Robert Redden Footbridge and Levee System – Pedestrian Walkway which connects downtown Rome with Heritage Park. Overlooks the levee system, which was built in 1939 by the U.S. Army corps of Engineers to prevent flooding of Rome.

HISTORIC AREAS

Barnsley Gardens – *A resort featuring an 18 hole championship golf course, full spa, swimming, tennis, walking trails and restaurants. The area includes the historic ruins of an 18th century plantation house. For information call 770 773-7480.*

Between the Rivers Historic District and Historic Downtown Rome – Features Rome's oldest homes, churches, restaurants and shops.

Carnegie Building – Funded by Andrew Carnegie as one of the original thirty libraries located in Georgia. Located at 603 Broad Street.

DeSoto Theatre – Built in 1929 , it is now home of the Rome Little Theater group. Located at 530 Broad Street.

Masonic Temple – Gothic Revival building located on downtown Broad Street. Built in 1871.

Historic Downtown Churches and Victorian Homes – Beautiful building and homes, many built in the eighteenth century.

Home-on-the-Hill, Alhambra -   One of the oldest structures in Northwest Georgia, this house was built in 1834-1837 by Philip W. Hemphill, one of the founders of Rome. Since 1923, the house has been occupied by the presidents of Darlington School, an independent, co-educational, boading and day school.   It located on Darlington Drive in Rome.

Cotton Block – Where cotton was warehoused, auctioned and shipped in the late 1800s. Located in downtown Rome.

Berry College – A four-year liberal arts college located on 28,000 acres of land, it is the largest campus in the world. For more information call 706 232-5374

Possum Trot - Original schoolhouse where Martha Berry began her teaching. Located on the campus of Berry College.

Old Mill Water Wheel – This Mill located on the campus of Berry College still produces corn meal once a year in celebration of Martha Berry's birthday.

Ford Complex – Beautiful complex built with funds donated by Henry Ford. Contains residential housing, classrooms and an auditorium. Located on the Berry College campus.

House of Dreams – Built by the students at Berry College in the early 1900's as a gift for Martha Berry. It is located atop Lavender Mountain.

Cave Spring – Picturesque city features ninety historic building and structures. The area is known throughout the state for its antique shops.

Shorter University – Four-year liberal arts college located on 150 acres. It is Rome's oldest College. For more information call 706 291-2121

Thornwood – Built by Colonel Alfred Shorter in 1847, Thornwood is at the intersection of Horseleg Creek Road and Shorter Ave. This home survived the Civil War, even though twice occupied by Federal Troops. It is now Darlington's Lower School , pre-K through grade 5.

PARKS AND RECREATIONAL AREAS

Hertiage Park and Confluence of Three Rivers. – Public Park located where the Oostanaula and Etowah rivers meet to form the Coosa River. Also the location of the Robert Redden Footbridge.

Ridge Ferry Park and Heritage Walking Trail - Fifty-four acre public park that includes walking and running paths along the Oostanula River.

Rocky Moutain Recration and Public Fishing Center - Camping, Fishing, Hunting, hiking, picnicking and beach area. Call 706 802-5087 for more information.

Lock and Dam Park – Seventy-three acre park featuring the lock and dam which was built in the early 1900's, but closed in 1941. This park provides some of the best fishing in Northwest Georgia, also camping and picnicking facilities. For more information call 706 234-5001.

Marshall Forest – a 250-acre forest which was Georgia's first National Natural Landmark. Features a Braille and wildflower trail and is managed by the Nature Conservancy. For more information call 706 291-2121.

Pocket Recreation Area – Public campground and picnic area located inside the Chattahoochee National Forest. Approximately two miles of walking trails in the park plus RV camping facilities. Directions: Hwy 27 N. to Hwy 156, left onto Floyd Springs Road, approx 12 miles. Information 706 236-5046.

Rome-Floyd Tennis Center – Public facility offers 16 lighted hard courts and a clubhouse with shower, lockers and concessions. For more information call 706-290-0072.

Rolater Park – 29-acre park listed on the National Register of Historic Places, includes a cave and fresh water spring. Excess spring water flows into a 1.5-acre size swimming pool shaped like the state of Georgia. For more information call 706 777-8439 Located in Cave Spring, Georgia.

POINTS OF INTEREST

Rome City Hall and Auditorium – Built in the early 1900's, and is the home of many local programs and performances, including the South's oldest symphony. Also serves as city Hall. Call 706 236-4400

Cedartown Performing Arts Center – Dedicated in 1976, the auditorium is located in the Cedartown Civic Complex. The theatre provides easy access and free parking and has more 940 plus seating capacity. For more information call 770 489-4168

Chief John Ross Pedestrian Bridge – Located downtown by the Forum. The bridge crosses over the Oostanaula River. It connects with the Town Green in front of the Forum.

Greater Rome Chamber of Commerce – Serves as Floyd County's Center for Business, Industry and Economic Development. Also the center for information on lodging, shopping, dining, and entertainment in the Greater Rome area. For more information call 706 291-7663. www.romega.com

The Forum Civic Center Complex – Multi-purpose convention and civic center located in the heart of downtown Rome. For more information call 706 291-5281.

Rome-Floyd County Library and Reading Gardens – Located on 7½ acres, this 75,000 square foot building houses over 250,000 books, special collections and audio/visual resources. For more information call 706 236-4600.

Friends of the Library Gift Shop – A member of the Museum Store Association, this shop is located at the main entrance of the library. The shop offers unique items and Greater Rome collectibles. For more information call 706-236-4637.

Rome Civic Center – 400 Civic Center Drive. For rental information call 706 236-4416

Richard B. Russell Regional Airport and Tower Field– Offers lighted runways, automated weather service, flight and sky-diving instruction as well as a modern terminal. For more information Call 706-295-7835.

Rome Visitors Center – The Center, housed in a 1901 train station with attached red caboose, , is open daily. It provides brochures and information on local attractions and events. The Center is located on Civic Center Hill, along with an early cotton gin, a 1847 lathe, and a Corliss steam enging. Visitors will also find the Boswell Cabin, a typical housing for a pioneer family between 1830 and 1850, here. For more information call 706 295-5576 or 800 444-1834.

Rome-Floyd Parks and Recreation Authority –Recreation Centers in Garden Lakes, Lindale, East Rome, and the Senior Adult Center on Kingston Road, the Recreation Authority is able to provide quality athletic, instructional, and leisure programs for all ages. They also supervise and maintain the parks and athletic fields in Rome-Floyd County. For more information call 706 291-0766

YMCA – Located on East Second Avenue, in Rome, the YMCA provides programs for all ages with the goal of "Putting Christian Principles into action through programs that build spirit, mind, and body for all." For program information call 706 232-2468.

PLACES TO PLAY

Golf -Stonebridge Golf Course – An 18-hole, 72 par, championship - caliber golf course. For more information call 706 236-5046.

Callier Springs Country Club - Callier Springs Road - 706 234-1691 (Public play week days only)

Class Par 3 Golf - 75 Huffacker Road – 706 234-3331

Etowah Public Driving Range – Public golf practice driving range located at Etowah Park. Open March - November, please call 706-291-0766.

Golf Practice Range - West Rome Golf Center - 40 Shorter Industrial Blvd 706 235-2266

Miniature Golf - Putt-Putt Golf And Games. 3349 Alabama Highway 706 235-2817

Tennis - Rome/Floyd Tennis Center - 300 West Third Street 706 290-0072
  Alto Park - Ten Lighted Courts-1014 Burnett Ferry Road
  Coosa Park - Two Lighted Courts -Krannet Drive
  Etowah Park - Lighted Courts -1325 Etowah Park
  Shannon Park - Four Lighted Courts-Highway 53
Tolbert Park - Two Courts - Charlton Street
For information on all of above call 706 291-0766

Swimming - Cave Spring Pool - Rolater Park Cave Spring 706 777-8435

North Side Swim Center - 485 Kingston Avenue – 706 802-0256

Rome YMCA - 810 E. 2nd Ave. – 706 232-2468

Camping - Cedar Creek Park - Highway 411 South - Cave Spring – 706 777-3030

Lock and Dam Park - Walker Mountain Road - Rome –706 234-5001

Rocky Mountain Recreation Area - Big Texas Valley Road –706 802-5087

Gunby Equestrian Center - Berry College – 706 236-2266

Sky Diving - Air Ventures Skydiving Center –304 Russell Field Rd. NE – 706 234-3097

Fishing and Boat Ramps - Call Rome/Floyd Recreation Authority - 300 West Third - 291-0766

AREA ENTERTAINMENT

Class Bowling Center - 75 Huffacker Road – 706 234-3323

Floyd Bowling & Amusement Center - 7 Riverbend Road – 706 234-7373

Etowah Skate Center - Highway 293 – 706 232-7498

Hot Wheels Skating Center - Highway 101 – 706 295-5867

Roller Kingdom - 2606 Calhoun Road – 706 291-7681

The Movies at Berry Square - Mount Berry Square – 706 235-9335

Rome Cinemas - 2535 Shorter Avenue – 706 236-4444

Village Theaters - 836 Turner McCall Blvd. – 706 235-7799

Aladdin's Castle - Mount Berry Square Mall - 295-4014

PLACES TO AVOID

Columbia Redmond Medical Center - 501 Redmond Road – 706 291-0291

Floyd Medical Center - 304 Turner McCall Blvd. – 706 802-2000

Harbin Clinic -1825 Martha Berry Blvd– 706 295-5331

PLACES TO LEARN

Berry College - 2277 Martha Berry Blvd, Mt. Berry, GA. – 706 232-5374

Georgia Highlands College - 3175 Cedartown Hwy. Rome, GA- 706 802-5000

Shorter University - 315 Shorter Ave. Rome, GA –706 291-2121 www.shorter.edu

Georgia Northwestern Technical College- Coosa Valley Technical Institute –785 Cedar Ave. Rome, GA 706 295-6963

Floyd County Schools - 600 Riverside Parkway N.E. Rome, GA 706 234-1031

Rome City Schools - - Central Office – 706 236-5050

Private Schools

Darlington School - 1014 - Cave Spring Rd. Rome, *706 235-6051*
www.darlingtonschool.org

St. Mary's Catholic School - 401-East 7th St. - 706 234-4953

Unity Christian School - 95 Burton Rd. – 706 292-0700

Berry Schools - Kindergarten through Eighth – 706 236-2242

Montessori School of Rome, 165 Dodd Blvd. – 706 232-7744

PLACES TO ENJOY

Rome Little Theatre - 530 Broad Street St. – 706 295-7171

Rome Symphony Guild - 538 Broad St. – 706 291-7067

The Forum Civic Center - 2 Government Plaza – 706 291-5281

Rome Area Council for the Arts – 706 295-2787

Rome Symphony Orchestra - 538 Broad St. – 706 291-7067

National Creative Society - 378-9144

ANNUAL EVENTS

Martin Luther King, Jr. Celebration - January – 706 235-5928

Atlanta Steeplechase - April - Kingston Downs – 706 295-5576

Confederate Veterans Day - April Myrtle Hill Cemetery – 706 234-8974

Herb & Plant Sale - April - Chieftains Museum – 706 291-9494

Mayfest on the Rivers - May – 706 291-0766

First Fridays Concerts - Downtown Rome – 706 295-5576

Showcase For The Arts - May – 706 291-2121

Silver Hills Rodeo - Memorial Day weekend – 706 212-7787

Farmers Market - Wed. & Sat Mornings - June - September – 706 291-0766

Cave Spring Arts Festival - Second weekend in June   706 777-8458

Salute to Honor America - Fourth of July – 706 291-0766

Cave Spring, Christmas in July - July -   Cave Spring 706 777-0523

Clocktower Road Race - August - Heritage Park – 706 232-2604

Armuchee Blue Grass Festival - Labor Day Weekend Armuchee, GA

Running Water PowWow - Labor Day weekend - Ridge Ferry Park

Coosa Valley Fair - October - Rome Fair Grounds –706 234-8771

Trout Unlimited Chili Cook-off - October - Ridge Ferry Park – 706 234-5310

Heritage Holidays - Third weekend in October – 706 291-0766

Chiaha Harvest Fair - Third or Fourth Weekend in October –706 235-4542

Peach State Marching Festival - Fourth weekend in October - Barron Stadium – 706 236-5082

John Wisdom Wagon Train Parade – Third weekend in October. 706 346-6623

Christmas in November - First Friday and Saturday in November

Telebration - Friday before Thanksgiving – 706 295-2787

Downtown Rome Christmas Parade - Tuesday after Thanksgiving – 706 295-5576

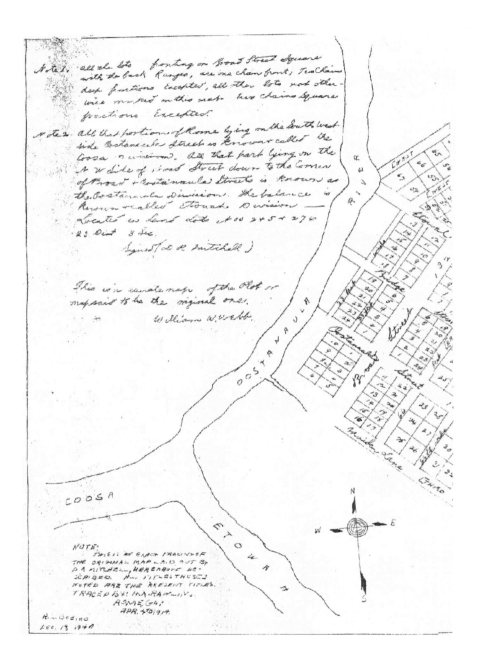

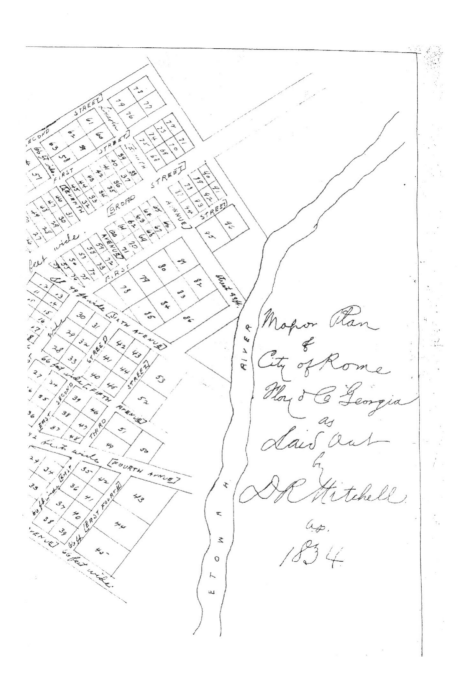

Made in the USA
Charleston, SC
28 January 2012